KT-525-387

Assessment for learning

Putting it into practice

*Paul Black, Christine Harrison, Clare Lee,
Bethan Marshall and Dylan Wiliam*

Open University Press

Trafford College
Library

Acc. No.	34936
Order No.	21683
Date	18.07.08

Open University Press
McGraw-Hill Education
McGraw-Hill House
Shoppenhangers Road
Maidenhead
Berkshire
England
SL6 2QL

email: enquiries@openup.co.uk
world wide web: www.openup.co.uk

and

Two Penn Plaza, New York, NY 10121 - 2289, USA

First published 2003

Reprinted 2004 (four times), 2005 (twice), 2006 (twice), 2007

Copyright © Paul Black et al. 2003

All rights reserved. Except for the quotation of short passages for the purpose of criticism and review, no part of this publication may be reproduced, stored in a retrieval system, or transmitted, in any form or by any means, electronic, mechanical, photocopying, recording or otherwise, without the prior written permission of the publisher or a licence from the Copyright Licensing Agency Limited. Details of such licences (for reprographic reproduction) may be obtained from the Copyright Licensing Agency Ltd of 90 Tottenham Court Road, London, W1T 4LP.

A catalogue record of this book is available from the British Library

ISBN 0 335 21297 2 (pb) 0 335 21298 0 (hb)
ISBN 13: 978 0 335 21297 2 (pb) 978 0 335 21298 9 (hb)

Library of Congress Cataloging-in-Publication Data
CIP data has been applied for

Typeset by RefineCatch Limited, Bungay, Suffolk
Printed in Poland EU by OZGraf. S.A.
www.polskabook.pl

NORTH TRAFFORD COLLEGE

00034936

7
Day
Loan

Ass
lea

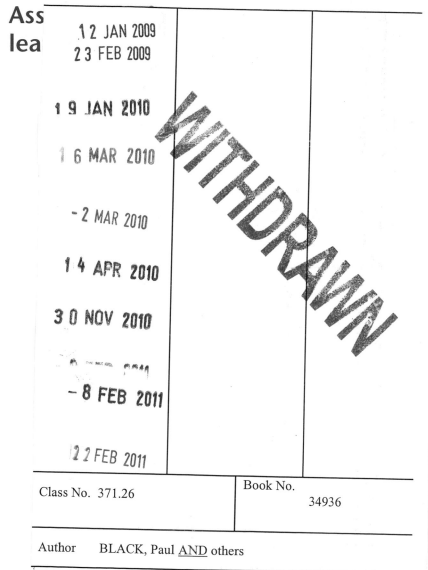

1 2 JAN 2009
2 3 FEB 2009

1 9 JAN 2010

1 6 MAR 2010

- 2 MAR 2010

1 4 APR 2010

3 0 NOV 2010

- 8 FEB 2011

2 2 FEB 2011

WITHDRAWN

Class No. 371.26

Book No.
34936

Author   BLACK, Paul AND others

Title
          Assessment for learning: Putting it into practice.

This book must be returned on or before the date shown above
Trafford College
Talbot Road Centre Stretford Manchester M32 0XH
Tel: 0161 886 7012

Contents

Acknowledgements

The origin of this work was an initiative of the Assessment Task Group of the British Educational Research Association (now known as the Assessment Reform Group). Their invitation to two of us (P.B. and D.W.) to review the research literature on formative assessment gave the initial impetus for the project with schools on which this book is based. We are grateful to them, but also to the Nuffield Foundation, who provided the support for the review and subsequently agreed to fund our project. We also acknowledge with pleasure the collaboration with Professor Myron Atkin and his colleagues at Stanford University and the funding provided by the US National Science Foundation through Stanford (NSF Grant REC-9909370), which enabled us to extend and broaden the range of our work.

We are indebted to the two local education authorities and their officers, notably Rose Collinson and Sue Swaffield from Medway and Dorothy Kavanagh from Oxfordshire, for their collaboration and support throughout the project. Through their efforts we were able to secure the commitment of the heads of six schools and to them we are also grateful. We acknowledge also the work of these officers and of representatives from the Department for Education and Skills and from the Qualifications and Assessment Authority, whose contributions in the project's steering group kept us in touch with many realities that we might otherwise have overlooked.

If this project has heroines and heroes, however, they are the forty-eight teachers of English, mathematics and science who took on the central and risky task of turning our ideas into practical working knowledge in their own classrooms. This project turned out to be far more productive and rewarding than we could ever have predicted: we are clear that the main reason for this lies in the commitment, to their educational ideals and professional values, that these teachers brought to their work with us.

The authors

Paul Black is Emeritus Professor at King's College. During his career he has been involved in a range of Nuffield curriculum projects and in many research projects, mainly in science education and in assessment. In 1987–88, he chaired the task group (TGAT) that advised ministers on the new national assessment and testing policy. Since his retirement he has concentrated on the study of formative assessment.

Chris Harrison taught science in several schools in the London area before she joined King's College in 1993. She now spends part of her time working with trainee teachers. Her work in formative assessment at King's has led to several professional development projects with teachers in the UK and abroad at both primary and secondary level. She has also worked on developing thinking skills in classrooms.

Clare Lee was the research fellow for the KMOFAP project. Previously she had taught secondary mathematics for over twenty years in several schools and researched, part-time, issues surrounding Teacher Action Research. Currently she is Teacher Adviser for Assessment for Warwickshire, leading the drive to establish Assessment for Learning within the LEA.

Bethan Marshall worked as an English teacher in London comprehensives for nine years before taking up her post at King's College. For five years she combined her post there with work as an English adviser. She is known for her writing and broadcasting on issues relating to English teaching and, latterly, on assessment issues.

Dylan Wiliam is Professor of Educational Assessment at King's. After several years teaching mathematics in London schools, he joined the college to work on a joint project with the ILEA to develop Graded Assessment in Mathematics as a new route to GCSE. He subsequently directed the first consortium to set the new key stage 3 national tests. He is well known for his work in both mathematics education and in assessment. He is currently an Assistant Principal of King's College.

1 Introduction
Why study this book?

This book is about changes in teachers' classroom practice that can make teaching and learning more effective. To be useful, such a book should be both practical, in giving concrete details and examples of classroom work, and principled, in giving a basis in both evidence and theory to underpin the practicalities. The authors of this book worked in a university and can lay claim to expertise in the areas of evidence and theory. The practical and concrete they have learnt in work with teachers, and the experiences, the evidence and the writing of these teachers is an important source for the work. So we are confident that teachers will benefit from taking our message seriously.

What is proposed?

What is proposed concerns assessment. This is not a simple or innocent term. Many take it to include all forms of testing. With this broad meaning, assessment can be seen to serve a range of purposes. One is to provide numerical results to publish in league tables – that is, the purpose is to help make schools *accountable*. Since this book is not concerned with assessments made for this purpose, we shall not discuss the controversies about the whole process (Black 1998; Wiliam 2001).

A second purpose is to provide students with *certificates*, such as GCSEs. The idea here is to give information about the students which they themselves, prospective employers and those controlling admission to further stages of education can use to make choices. This purpose calls for assessment methods which can be reliable, in that they are comparable across different schools, and indeed across the country as a whole, and also valid in that they give the users what they really need to know about each student. These are exacting requirements, but again assessments made for this purpose are not the main focus of this book.

As our title makes clear, this book is about a third purpose – *assessment for learning*. The focus here is on any assessment for which the first priority is to serve the purpose of promoting students' learning. It thus differs from the purposes described above. For the league tables or the GCSEs, the main assessment methods are formal tests: these usually, although not inevitably, involve tests that are infrequent, isolated from normal teaching and learning, carried out on special occasions with formal rituals, and often conducted by methods over which individual teachers have little or no control. Assessment for learning is not like this at all – it is usually informal, embedded in all aspects of teaching and learning, and conducted by different teachers as part of their own diverse and individual teaching styles.

An assessment activity can help learning if it provides information to be used as feedback by teachers, and by their students in assessing themselves and each other, to modify the teaching and learning activities in which they are engaged. Such assessment becomes *formative assessment* when the evidence is used to adapt the teaching work to meet learning needs.

Formative assessment can occur many times in every lesson. It can involve several different methods for encouraging students to express what they are thinking and several different ways of acting on such evidence. It has to be within the control of the individual teacher and, for this reason, change in formative assessment practice is an integral and intimate part of a teacher's daily work.

Why take formative assessment seriously?

Evidence of surveys of teacher practice shows that formative assessment is not at present a strong feature of classroom work. It follows that to establish good formative assessment practices in classrooms requires that most teachers make significant changes. Any non-trivial change in classroom teaching involves the teacher both in taking risks and, at least during the process of change, in extra work. We are confident, however, that teachers will find it worth their while to take on the changes that are involved in improving formative assessment, for the following reasons:

- There is ample evidence that the changes involved will raise the scores of their students on normal conventional tests.
- The changes involved have been shown to be feasible – that is, teachers have been able to incorporate them successfully in their normal classroom work.
- The work involved turns out to be a redistribution of effort: the message is not about working harder, but about working smarter.

- The changes can be made step by step – a big 'leap in the dark' is not necessary.
- Teachers come to enjoy their work more and to find it more satisfying because it resonates with their professional values.
- They also see that their students come to enjoy, understand and value their learning more as a result of the innovations.

These are bold claims. One purpose of this book is to explain the evidence and experience upon which they are based. Part of that evidence comes from existing books and research papers that recount the work of many groups from around the world. However, the major part comes from the experience of a group of teachers in six schools. In collaboration with us, these teachers have worked out, over the two and a half years of the project's work, how to implement reforms in their formative assessment. Their experience, our observations of their work and their reflections on the changes they have made are the bedrock for this book.

In particular, the claim that test scores can be raised by methods which teachers find professionally rewarding is based on the test results of this group of teachers, whether from their schools' normal tests, from key stage tests or from GCSE examinations. The teachers showed extraordinary commitment to this work, although this commitment was in part fuelled by the rewarding nature of the classroom work that they experienced. Apart from day release for twelve one-day meetings, they did not have any concessions to reduce their normal teaching load.

How this book tells its story

The content of this book is in part a story of our work in schools and in part a reflection on the lessons we infer from that story. As Figure 1.1 illustrates, there are three main themes, outlined as follows:

Overview

Chapter 2 describes lessons learned from an extensive survey of the relevant research literature which was completed in 1997, and published alongside the booklet *Inside the Black Box* (Black and Wiliam 1998a,b). The chapter sets out the principles, derived from this survey, on which the work with schools was based. Chapter 8 is a closing reflection. It will summarize the main lessons. It will also reflect on what we have learnt about making an impact, particularly in both highlighting and contributing to the most important debate of all, which is the debate about the improvement of the learning of students and of

OVERVIEW   IMPLEMENTATION   PRACTICE

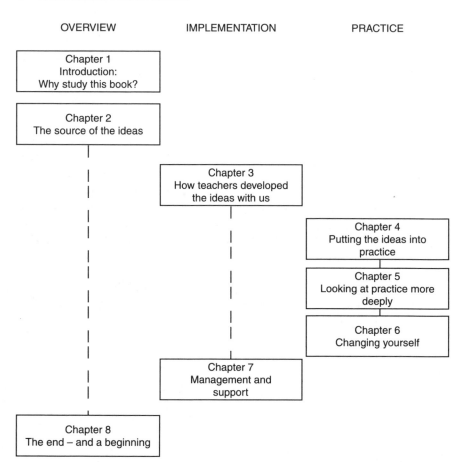

Figure 1.1   An outline of the book: three main strands.

their capacity to learn in the future. That is, it is about the core activity of all schools.

Implementation

Chapter 3 describes how we went about putting ideas into practice with six schools and the forty-eight teachers of English, mathematics and science involved. It also sets out the evidence about the significant learning gains that these teachers achieved. Chapter 7 returns to this theme by exploring ways in which, given the findings presented in this book, schools and those advising and supporting them might plan to implement formative practices.

Practice

Chapters 4, 5 and 6 are the heart of this book. They discuss the lessons learnt in practice from three perspectives. Chapter 4 sets out the concrete activities that the teachers developed as they transformed ideas about formative assessment into practical working knowledge. Chapter 5 looks at these activities from more fundamental perspectives, reflecting on them in terms of the principles of learning and of motivation that are entailed, and exploring also the similarities and differences between practices in different school subjects. Such reflections are prompted by our experience that changes in formative assessment practices, far from being just a set of useful tactical changes in classroom learning, have turned out to be far more significant and far more radical in their effects. Chapter 6 adopts a more personal and individual perspective, describing the experience of teachers as individuals as they worked to change both their approach to fundamentals of teaching and learning and their beliefs about these fundamentals. All three of these chapters draw upon the experiences and writing of the teachers involved. Apart from the three long pieces in Chapter 6, all references to teachers and their schools are pseudonyms.

Those mainly interested in practical application in their classrooms might concentrate on the three chapters on practice; those who look for ways to disseminate the practices will want to read Chapters 3 and 7 as well; while study of Chapters 1, 5 and 6 will help a reader to see the developments from a more fundamental and theoretical perspective. Chapters 2–6 draw mainly on our own work, especially our work with schools. In Chapter 7, we provide ideas from a wider range of sources.

2 The source of the ideas

Introduction

Although some of us have been interested in formative assessment for over 20 years, the origin of the work on formative assessment that is described here was the review by Black and Wiliam (1998a). This review covered a very wide range of published research and provided evidence that formative assessment raises standards and that current practices are weak. However, there was little to help teachers put the research findings into practice. This was followed by the booklet *Inside the Black Box* (Black and Wiliam 1998b), which served four aims:

- The first was to give a brief review of the research evidence.
- The second was to make a case for more attention to be paid to helping practice inside the classroom.
- The third was to draw out implications for practical action.
- The fourth was to discuss policy and practice.

This chapter will concentrate on the first two of these aims. The third has been the main aim of our work since 1998 and is the main theme of later chapters of this book. The fourth will be looked at only briefly in the closing chapter.

The research evidence

The review by Black and Wiliam (1998a) involved studying reviews of research published up to 1988 and then checking through the issues of over 160 research journals and books for the years 1988 to 1997. This process yielded about 681 articles or chapters to study. The seventy-page review drew on material from 250 of these sources. One of the priorities in evaluating the research reports was to identify and summarize studies that produced quantitative evidence that innovations in formative assessment can lead to improvement in the learning of students. Brief accounts of four such studies will serve here to give the flavour of the evidence.

The first was a project in which twenty-five Portuguese teachers of mathematics were trained in self-assessment methods on a 20-week part-time course, methods which they put into practice, as the course progressed, with their students – 246 of them aged 8 and 9 years (Fernandes and Fontana 1996). The students of a further twenty Portuguese teachers who were taking another course in education at the time served as a control group. Both the experimental and the control groups of students were given the same pre- and post-tests of mathematics achievement, and both spent the same amount of time in class on mathematics. Both groups showed significant gains over the period, but the experimental group's mean gain was about twice that of the control group – a clearly significant difference. Similar effects were obtained for some older students.

The focus of the assessment work was on regular – mainly daily – self-assessment by the students. However, this focus meant that the students also had to be taught to understand both the learning objectives and the assessment criteria; they were also given the opportunity to choose learning tasks and to use these in assessing their own learning outcomes. Thus the initiative involved far more than simply adding some assessment exercises to existing teaching. So this research raised a question: whether it is possible to introduce formative assessment without some radical change in classroom pedagogy because, of its nature, this type of assessment is an essential component of classroom learning.

The second example was itself a review of twenty-one different studies, of children ranging from pre-school to grade 12 (Fuchs and Fuchs 1986). The main focus was on work for children with mild disabilities, and on the use of the feedback to and by teachers. The studies were carefully selected – all involved comparison between experimental and control groups, and all involved assessment activities with frequencies of between two and five times per week. For each study, the authors first calculated the difference between the gain in scores of the experimental over the control group, and then divided this figure by a measure of the spread of the scores across the children of either group. They did this because they could use this ratio, which is known as the 'effect size', to compare different studies with one another. The overall mean of the effect sizes was 0.73 for handicapped children and 0.63 for the non-handicapped. Where teachers worked with systematic procedures to review the assessments and take action accordingly, the mean effect size was 0.92, whereas where action was not systematic it was 0.42.

Two features of this last example are of particular interest. The first is that the authors compared the striking success of the interactive (i.e. formative), approach with the unsatisfactory outcomes of projects which used diagnostic pre-tests only as a filter to assign children to pre-prepared individual learning programmes. The second feature was that the main learning gains from the formative work were only achieved when teachers were constrained to use the data in systematic ways, ways which were new to them.

The third example was undertaken with 5-year-old children (Bergan *et al.* 1991). It involved 838 children drawn mainly from disadvantaged home backgrounds in six different regions in the USA. The teachers of the experimental group were trained to implement a system that required an initial assessment to inform teaching at the individual pupil level, consultation on progress after 2 weeks, new assessments to give a further diagnostic review and new decisions about students' needs after 4 weeks, with the whole course lasting 8 weeks. There was emphasis in their training on observations of skills to assess progress, on a criterion-referenced model of the development of understanding and on diagnostic assessments designed to help locate each child at a point on this model. Progress in reading, in mathematics and in science in the experimental group was considerably greater than in the control group even though the tests used were multiple-choice and not well suited to the child-centred style of the experimental group. Furthermore, of the control group, on average 1 child in 3.7 was referred as having particular learning needs and 1 in 5 was placed in special education; the corresponding figures for the experimental group were 1 in 17 and 1 in 71.

The researchers concluded that the capacity of children is under-developed in conventional teaching so that many are 'put down' unnecessarily. One feature of the experiment's success was that teachers had enhanced confidence in their powers to make referral decisions wisely. This example illustrates again the embedding of a rigorous formative assessment routine within an innovative programme linked to a criterion-based scheme of diagnostic assessment.

The fourth example was a study of an inquiry-based middle-school science curriculum module (White and Frederiksen 1998) that was focused on a practical inquiry approach to learning. There were twelve classes of thirty students each in two schools. Each class was taught to the same curriculum plan and all students worked in peer groups. A control group of classes spent part of the classroom time on a general discussion of the module, while an experimental group spent the same length of time on discussion structured to promote reflective assessment, with both peer assessment of presentations to the class and self-assessment. All students were given the same basic skills test at the outset. On comparison of the scores gained on their projects, the experimental group showed a significant overall gain. However, when the students were divided into groups according to low, medium or high scores on the initial basic skills test, the low scorers were better than the control group by more than three standard deviations, the medium scorers by just over two standard deviations, and the high scorers by just over one standard deviation. A similar pattern, of superiority of the experimental group, was also found for scores on a test of the physics concepts. For students in the experimental group, those who showed the best understanding of the assessment process achieved the highest scores.

Here again the formative assessment was built into an innovation to change teaching and learning. Three features stand out: the use of 'reflective assessment' in peer groups, the use of several outcome measures all directly reflecting the aims of the teaching, and the fact that the intervention was most effective for the lowest attaining students.

In all, about twenty relevant studies were found: the second example described above (by Fuchs and Fuchs 1986) was one of the twenty and itself reviewed twenty-one studies, so in effect the body of evidence included over forty studies. All of these studies showed that innovations that include strengthening the practice of formative assessment produce significant, and often substantial, learning gains. The studies ranged over ages (from 5-year-olds to university undergraduates), across several school subjects and over several countries. The mean effect sizes for most of these studies were between 0.4 and 0.7: such effect sizes are among the largest ever reported for sustained educational interventions. The following examples illustrate some practical consequences of such large gains:

- An effect size of 0.4 would mean that the average (i.e. at the 50th percentile) pupil involved in an innovation would move up to the same achievement as a pupil at the 35th percentile (i.e. almost in the top third) of those not involved.
- A gain of effect size 0.5 would improve performances of students in GCSE by at least one grade.
- A gain of effect size 0.7, if realized in international comparative studies in mathematics (TIMSS; Beaton *et al.* 1996), would raise England from the middle of the forty-one countries involved into the top five.

Some, but not all, of the studies showed that improved formative assessment helped the (so-called) low attainers more than the rest, and so reduced the spread of attainment while also raising it overall. Any gains for such students could be particularly important: they show that the 'tail' of low educational achievement might be due, at least in part, to failure to develop the potential talents of the 'weaker' student.

It therefore seemed clear that very significant learning gains might be achievable. The fact that such gains had been achieved by a variety of methods, which had, as a common feature, enhanced formative assessment, indicated that it is this feature which accounted, at least in part, for the successes. It also showed that the positive outcomes might not depend on the fine details of any particular innovation. However, it did not follow that it would be an easy matter to achieve such gains on a wide scale in normal classrooms. The research reports did bring out, between and across them, other features that appeared to characterize many of the studies:

- All of them involved new ways to enhance feedback between those taught and the teacher, ways which required new modes of pedagogy and therefore significant changes in classroom practice.
- Underlying the various approaches were assumptions about what makes for effective learning – in particular that students have to be actively involved.
- For assessment to function formatively, the results had to be used to adjust teaching and learning – so a significant aspect of any pro- gramme would be the ways in which teachers do this.
- The ways in which assessment affected the motivation and self- esteem of students, and the benefits of engaging students in self- assessment, both deserved careful attention.

Current practice

The second feature of the research review was to look for research evidence about the quality of the everyday practice of assessment in classrooms. This evidence showed that such practice was beset with problems and shortcom- ings, as the following quotations indicate:

> Marking is usually conscientious but often fails to offer guidance on how work can be improved. In a significant minority of cases, marking reinforces under-achievement and under-expectation by being too generous or unfocused. Information about pupil perform- ance received by the teacher is insufficiently used to inform sub- sequent work.
>
> (General report on secondary schools – OFSTED 1996)

> Why is the extent and nature of formative assessment in science so impoverished?
>
> (UK secondary science teachers – Daws and Singh 1996)

> The criteria used were 'virtually invalid by external standards'.
>
> (French primary teachers – Grisay 1991)

> Indeed they pay lip service to it but consider that its practice is unrealistic in the present educational context.
>
> (Canadian secondary teachers – Dassa *et al.* 1993).

The most important difficulties, which were found in the UK but also elsewhere, could be briefly divided into three groups. The first was concerned with *effective learning*:

- Teachers' tests encourage rote and superficial learning; this is seen even where teachers say they want to develop understanding – and many appear unaware of the inconsistency.
- The questions and other methods used are not discussed with or shared between teachers in the same school, and they are not critically reviewed in relation to what they actually assess.
- For primary teachers in particular, there is a tendency to emphasize quantity and presentation of work and to neglect its quality in relation to learning.

The second group was concerned with *negative impact*:

- The giving of marks and the grading functions are over-emphasized, while the giving of useful advice and the learning function are under-emphasized.
- The use of approaches in which students are compared with one another, the prime purpose of which appears to them to be competition rather than personal improvement. In consequence, assessment feedback teaches students with low attainments that they lack 'ability', so they are de-motivated, believing that they are not able to learn.

The third group focused on the *managerial role* of assessments:

- Teachers' feedback to students often appears to serve social and managerial functions, often at the expense of the learning functions.
- Teachers are often able to predict students' results on external tests – because their own tests imitate them – but at the same time they know too little about their students' learning needs.
- The collection of marks to fill up records is given greater priority than the analysis of students' work to discern learning needs; furthermore, some teachers pay no attention to the assessment records of previous teachers of their students.

Of course, not all of these descriptions apply now to all classrooms and, indeed, there will be many schools and classrooms to which they do not apply. Nevertheless, these general conclusions were drawn by authors in several countries, including the UK, who had collected evidence by observation, interviews and questionnaires from many schools.

Planning further work

The need

Overall, the research review of Black and Wiliam (1998a) attracted widespread attention in the academic world. The whole of the journal issue in which it appeared was devoted to the topic, the review article being followed by six articles, each of about ten pages, in which experts in the field from the USA, Australia, Switzerland and South Africa commented on the review. Although these added many valuable insights, none of them challenged its main findings.

For the world of professional practice, the booklet *Inside the Black Box* and the article based on it published in a US journal, met its overall aim of attracting attention and raising debate. Its success in this respect is evidence of the importance of the issues raised, and of the fact that the message speaks to the basic professional concerns of very many teachers. It has been widely quoted in policy and professional circles and at the time of writing has sold over 40,000 copies.

The obvious question raised by the nature of the message and the evidence of positive impact was whether any follow-up action should be taken. Innovations in formative assessment had already been undertaken and reported in the literature before 1998. Apart from those directly concerned with the issue, formative feedback was also a feature in several other innovations, notably mastery learning, assessment by portfolios, curriculum-based assessment and cognitively guided instruction. It did not seem feasible, however, to attempt to replicate any of these in UK schools working within the constraints of the national curriculum and assessment. So any action would have to be based on a selection of those ideas in the research literature which appeared to be both feasible and potentially productive.

A key reservation about any such action was expressed in the following passage from *Inside the Black Box*:

> Teachers will not take up attractive sounding ideas, albeit based on extensive research, if these are presented as general principles which leave entirely to them the task of translating them into everyday practice – their classroom lives are too busy and too fragile for this to be possible for all but an outstanding few. What they need is a variety of living examples of implementation, by teachers with whom they can identify and from whom they can both derive conviction and confidence that they can do better, and see concrete examples of what doing better means in practice.
> (Black and Wiliam 1998b, pp. 15–16; emphasis in original)

Thus any ideas, however promising, derived from the research would have to be tried out in practice.

The basis

The research review did set out some of the issues that any programme of development might have to face. These were concerned with teacher change, students' perspectives and the central concept of feedback, respectively.

The problem of 'teacher change' was emphasized in several of the research reports. There was evidence of patchy implementation of reforms of teacher assessment in France (Broadfoot *et al.* 1996) and in Canada (Dassa 1990), while in the UK some changes had produced a diversity of practices, some of which appeared to be counter-productive and in conflict with the stated aims of the changes that triggered them (McCallum *et al.* 1993; Gipps *et al.* 1997). Where changes had been introduced with substantial training or as an intrinsic part of a project in which teachers had been closely involved, the pace of change was often slow – it was very difficult for teachers to change practices that were closely embedded within their whole pattern of pedagogy (Torrie 1989; Shepard *et al.* 1994, 1996; Shepard 1995) and many lacked the interpretive frameworks required to coordinate the many separate bits of assessment information in the light of broad learning purposes (Bachor and Anderson 1994). A project with teachers in the creative arts, which tried to train them to communicate with students to appreciate the students' view of their own work, found that despite the training many teachers stuck to their own agenda and failed to respond to cues or clues from the students that could have re-oriented that agenda (Radnor 1994). In a project aimed at enhancing the power of science teachers to observe their students' at work, teachers could not find time for observing because they were not prepared to change classroom practices to give students more free responsibility and give themselves a less closely demanding control – the authors interpreted this as a reluctance to break the existing symbiosis of mutual dependency between teachers and students (Cavendish *et al.* 1990).

The main issue that emerged from such studies is that there are close links between formative assessment practice, the other components of a teacher's own pedagogy and a teacher's conception of his or her role. It followed that implementation of changes in classroom assessment would call for rather deep changes both in teachers' perceptions of their own role in relation to their students and in their classroom practice. It was also evident that the context of national or local requirements for certification and accountability exerted a powerful – usually harmful – influence on assessment practice.

For 'students' perspectives', the central problem was clearly expressed by Perrenoud:

A number of pupils do not aspire to learn as much as possible, but are content to 'get by', to get through the period, the day or the year without any major disaster, having made time for activities other than school work [. . .] Formative assessment invariably presupposes a shift in this equilibrium point towards more school work, a more serious attitude to learning [. . .] Every teacher who wants to practise formative assessment *must reconstruct the teaching contracts so as to counteract the habits acquired by his pupils.* Moreover, some of the children and adolescents with whom he is dealing are imprisoned in the identity of a bad pupil and an opponent.

(Perrenoud 1991, p. 92; emphasis in the original)

This rather pessimistic view was supported by several research studies. Some students might be reluctant to participate in any change not only because of a wish to minimize effort, but also because of fear and insecurity. Another problem is that students might fail to recognize formative feedback as a helpful signal and guide (Tunstall and Gipps 1996). Overall, a student's beliefs about learning were important in forming these responses. Issues of confidence, in oneself as a learner, and of motivation would serve to trigger the adoption of a negative response to change.

That these considerations would be central was indicated by the theoretical position of Sadler (1989). He pointed out that the core of the activity of formative assessment lies in the sequence of two actions. The first is the perception by the learner of a gap between a desired goal and his or her present state (of knowledge and/or understanding and/or skill). The second is the action taken by the learner to close that gap to attain the desired goal. The learner first has to understand the evidence about this gap and then take action on the basis of that evidence. Although the teacher can stimulate and guide this process, the learning has to be done by the student. It would be a mistake to regard the student as the passive recipient of any call to action: there are complex links between the way in which a message is understood, the way in which that perception motivates a selection among different courses of action, and the learning activity that might follow. These arguments made it clear theoretically that the development of self-assessment by the student might have to be an important feature of any programme of formative assessment, a point that had already been illustrated in several of the research studies.

The third key idea was the concept of 'feedback'. This concept deals with a feature central to the operation of any system that has to adapt to manage change. The key components in the operation of feedback of any such system are:

- data on the actual level of some measurable attribute;
- data on the desirable level of that attribute;

- a mechanism for comparing the two levels and assessing the gap between them;
- a mechanism by which the information can be used to alter the gap.

With small changes of terminology, the above four steps could be a description of formative assessment. The last of these components is essential: if the information is not actually used in altering the gap, then there is no feedback. It is also clear that the quality of the feedback provided is a key feature in any procedure for formative assessment.

One of the most important reviews of the effectiveness of feedback was carried out by Kluger and DeNisi (1996). They reviewed numerous reports of the effects of feedback on performance and, after excluding those which did not meet their stringent criteria of quality, were left with 131 reports, yielding 607 effect sizes and involving 12,652 participants. They found an average effect size of 0.4, but the standard deviation of the effect sizes was almost 1 and about two effects in every five were negative. However, their definition of feedback required only the collection and reporting of the data. Where the procedures also involved ways of using the data to make improvements, the effects were all positive. The explanation of this difference is that when people are only told that they have done well or badly, it will affect their ego but it is not likely to improve their involvement with their tasks (this issue is discussed in detail in Chapters 4 and 5).

The prospects

The principles to do with teacher change, student change and feedback would clearly have to be borne in mind in any innovative development. While these pointed to several theoretical ideas that would be relevant, notably those concerned with theories of learning, theories of motivation and Sadler's analysis of the role of feedback, there was no comprehensive theory that could form a basis for action.

At the more directly relevant level of strategies and tactics for classroom work, the literature indicated that the choice of learning tasks, the quality of questioning, classroom discourse and the orientation of feedback on oral and written work, self- and peer-assessment and the use of tests were all issues that could demand attention. However, for none of these could one confidently set out a recipe for improvement, not least because their implementation within any comprehensive framework, and within UK classrooms, had not been studied.

Underlying these reservations was a more general caution about the 'transfer' of innovations, however well researched, into the daily practice of teachers. The mere collection and publication of research data is not enough, as was made clear in the following extract from *Inside the Black Box*:

> *Thus the improvement of formative assessment cannot be a simple matter. There is no 'quick fix' that can be added to existing practice with promise of rapid reward.* On the contrary, if the substantial rewards of which the evidence holds out promise are to be secured, this will only come about if each teacher finds his or her own ways of incorporating the lessons and ideas that are set out above into her or his own patterns of classroom work. This can only happen relatively slowly, and through sustained programmes of professional development and support. This does not weaken the message here – indeed, it should be a sign of its authenticity, for lasting and fundamental improvements in teaching and learning can only happen in this way.
>
> (Black and Wiliam 1998b, p. 15; emphasis in original)

Such arguments raised the wider issues of the transfer of research results into professional practice and of the nature of the involvement of teachers in such work. It was concluded that what was needed was to set up a group of schools, each committed to the development of formative assessment. In such a process, the teachers in their classrooms would be working out the answers to many of the practical questions that the research literature could not answer, and reformulating the issues, perhaps in relation to fundamental insights, but certainly in terms which could make sense to their peers in ordinary class-rooms. It was envisaged that in such a programme the schools involved would need extra support, both to give their teachers time – to plan the initiative in the light of existing evidence, to reflect on their experience as it developed and to advise on training work for others in the future. In addition, there would be a need to support external evaluators to work with the teachers to help their development of the work and to collect evidence about its effectiveness. Such evidence would both help guide policy implementation and to disseminate findings to others.

In summary, it could be claimed that a firm case for a development programme had been made and that a basis for such a programme had been laid. However, it was equally clear that although the signpost had been set up on a road worth following, this work was only a first step along that road.

3   How teachers developed the ideas with us

The starting point

Given our commitment to undertaking development work to determine how formative assessment could be incorporated more effectively into professional practice, we had to find partners – local education authorities (LEAs), schools and teachers willing to take part in such a venture. We started by holding joint discussions with assessment advisory staff from Oxfordshire and Medway, chosen because we knew that key members of their LEA advisory staff would understand and support our approach and so might be willing to enter into a project with us. Thus Dorothy Kavanagh in Oxford and Rose Collinson and Sue Swaffield in Medway joined us in discussions which led to production of an agreed detailed plan. However, while they and a selection of their schools could take on the load of engaging in the work, and could commit some days of work of their advisory staff so that each authority would be fully involved, financial support was needed to release teachers for meetings and to make research staff available to observe and analyse the progress of the work.

So the next step was to make an application to the Nuffield Foundation for funding of a project. The proposal that we submitted to them set out the aims, the roles of the partners to be involved, the assumptions lying behind our approach and the timetable for the project.

The proposal and the partners

Our overall aims were to develop the implementation of formative assessment in the normal professional practices of teachers and to explore the advantages of such implementation. A related aim was to lay a basis for the design of programmes for wider dissemination of the findings and in particular to design in-service training (INSET) to replicate the implementation. The project method was to carry out an interactive INSET development programme involving three groups of partners: the teachers and their senior staff in the schools, staff at King's and the LEA advisory staff.

The role of the teachers was to plan and then to implement individual innovations in their classrooms, and then to help evaluate these, particularly by reflecting on their experience in developing formative assessment. The role envisaged for the staff at King's was, at the outset, to present ideas to the teachers and help them in designing and implementing their own innovations. Subsequently, they were to support and evaluate the processes of implementation and to use the findings in the design of dissemination and INSET work. Finally, the role envisaged for the advisory staff of the local authorities was, at the outset, to take the lead in the selection of the sample schools and in the negotiations with those selected. Subsequently, they were to share with the King's staff in the work of support, evaluation and dissemination

The proposal – assumptions

We thought it important to spell out, in our proposal, the main assumptions on which the project would be founded and organized. The first assumption was that existing research evidence had already established that development of formative assessment could produce substantial improvements in the learning of students and there was no need to repeat such work. However, there was a need to study how different teachers might realize such improvements within the normal constraints of curriculum and external testing requirements. We believed that any attempt to force adoption of a simple recipe by all teachers would not be effective, and that success would depend on how each could work out his or her own way of implementing change.

We judged nevertheless that existing research did provide some important guidance that would be helpful for all teachers. In particular, promotion of self-assessment by students, as a component of strategies to develop their capacity to take responsibility for their own learning, should be fundamental to the development of productive formative assessment. Part of our task would be to initiate the work by distilling and conveying such messages.

The Nuffield Foundation accepted the proposal with one reservation. We had not envisaged collecting any quantitative evidence of learning gains, since we judged that there was already adequate evidence that such gains could be achieved. However, the Foundation's referees advised that such quantitative evidence would be necessary to avoid the charge of 'but will it work here?', given that much (in fact, almost all) of the evidence cited by Black and Wiliam (1998a) was from outside the UK. So we agreed to collect quantitative evidence. This part of the project is described in the last section of this chapter.

The project started work in earnest in January 1999 and the funding supported work up to the end of the 1999–2000 school year. However, we subsequently entered into negotiation with colleagues at the School of Education in Stanford University who wished to develop a similar project with schools in California. They succeeded in obtaining funding for this from the US National Science Foundation. The King's team and the work in our schools were included in the project so that we were able to continue with full support until the summer of 2001. The contribution from King's was to inform the development at Stanford on the basis of our experience, and to develop further evidence in our schools about the dissemination of the project and about the interface between formative and summative assessment practices in our schools. We shall not in this book discuss the work in California.

The schools and teachers involved

Our proposal was that we would work with science and mathematics teachers. We believed that the detailed working out of new approaches would be different according to the nature of the school subjects. We therefore considered it likely that limited effort would best be invested in no more than two subjects – the two chosen were those in which the staff involved at King's had extensive experience. Earlier work at King's, notably in the Assessment of Performance in Science (APU; Black 1990), in the development of graded assessments in science (GASP project; Swain 1988) and in mathematics (GAIM projects; Brown 1989), and in work on assessment practices with science teachers (Fairbrother *et al.* 1994) provided important resources here. The experience with GASP and GAIM was that teachers achieved marked improvements in their assessment work, but that for many these were implemented only as frequent summative assessment. We thought that the obstacles that prevented many from achieving improvement in formative assessment could, in the light of our studies of existing research, be better understood so that we could foresee ways in which the new project could attempt to overcome these obstacles.

This restriction to areas in which we had extensive expertise also led us to work only in secondary schools. We could foresee that primary teachers, who guide the learning of students over a range of different subjects, would have problems and opportunities in formative assessment quite different from those of secondary teachers, and that these would have to be studied in a separate project.

For the secondary phase, we also envisaged that the work would be confined to years 7, 8 and 10 (i.e. to ages 11–12, 12–13 and 14–15 years). This was because it was likely that the pressure of external 'high-stakes' assessments would inhibit the development of formative assessment, and so the 'pressured' years 9 (key stage 3 testing) and 11 (GCSE) should be avoided. It was nevertheless clear that the interplay of the formative and summative assessments would be a factor in every year, but we judged that we might study this in those years when the summative aspects were largely within the control of each school. In the event, as will be clear later, this limitation could not be applied in practice.

The funding and the workload were planned in terms of the involvement of six schools, three each in the Oxfordshire and Medway authorities. The selection of the schools was left entirely in the hands of our LEA partners, but there was mutual agreement beforehand that the schools should:

- have some staff who were already keenly aware of assessment problems and thereby were prepared to take on fresh initiatives in this aspect of their work;
- be comprehensive maintained schools, either 11–16 or 11–18, and thus non-selective: the selection in Medway avoided grammar schools, but the existence of these did affect the intake of schools that were included;
- be schools with 'average' performance in public examination results, i.e. avoiding those with either privileged students or those with comparatively poor performance;
- form a sample of schools, which, taken together, would cover a range of types of catchment areas.

In the event, the six schools selected satisfied these conditions. Two were single-sex schools, one of girls and one of boys; the other four were mixed. In each participating school, two science teachers and two mathematics teachers were to work in the project. Commitment to support the project by the senior management team of each school was to be essential, and the heads of the departments of science and of mathematics would also have to be supportive, if not directly involved.

In the choice of teachers, as with the choice of schools, the King's team played no part. Teachers in each school were selected in a variety of ways. Some included a head of department together with a teacher in their first or second year of teaching. In some cases, teachers appeared to be selected because, in the words of one head, 'they could do with a bit of inset'. In the event, while our schools could not be designed by us to be representative, there was a considerable range of expertise and experience among the twenty-four teachers selected.

The way it went

Before the work of the project started, three of us (P.B., C.H. and D.W.) visited each school with the LEA officer to discuss the project with the headteacher and other members of the senior management team. All six schools identified agreed to be involved and so the King's Medway Oxford Formative Assessment Project (KMOFAP) was born.

At the outset, the plan was to work in a genuinely collaborative way with a small group of teachers, suggesting directions that might be fruitful to explore and supporting them as well as we could, but avoiding the trap of dispensing 'tips for teachers'. At first, it appeared that the teachers did not believe this. They seemed to believe that the researchers were operating with a perverted model of discovery learning in which the researchers know full well what they want the teachers to do, but don't tell them, because they want the teachers 'to discover it for themselves'. However, after a while it became clear that there was no prescribed model of effective classroom action, and each teacher would need to find their own way of implementing the general principles in their own classrooms.

The INSETs

The interaction between the King's team and the schools was developed in two main ways. One was by a series of INSET events which brought the team, the teachers and the LEA advisers together, the other was by visits of team members from King's to each school. The planning and progress were kept under review by a steering group composed of the LEA advisers, the King's team and representatives from the Department of Education and Skills (DfES), the Qualifications and Curriculum Authority (QCA), and the Teacher Training Agency (TTA).

There were eleven full- and one half-day INSETs. The original plan was to hold mainly half-day INSETS in each LEA to reduce the teachers' travelling time. In the event, only one such LEA-based session was held, because the teachers felt that they gained a great deal from working with teachers in the other authority. So all but one of these events took the form of a full-day session (typically 10 am to 4 pm). The Nuffield funding covered the cost of the first six-and-a-half days and the subsequent funding from the link with Stanford enabled extension beyond June 2000 for a further five. The sessions can be described as a sequence of three main phases as follows.

The key feature of the three sessions in the first phase, from February to September 1999, was the development of action plans. Since we were aware from other studies that effective implementation of formative assessment requires teachers to re-negotiate the 'learning contract' (cf. Brousseau 1984) that they had evolved with their students, we decided that implementing formative assessment would best be done at the beginning of a new school year. For the first 6 months of the project, therefore, we encouraged the teachers to experiment with some of the strategies and tactics suggested by the research, such as rich questioning, comment-only marking, sharing criteria with learners, and student peer- and self-assessment. Each teacher was then asked to draw up, and later to refine, an action plan specifying which aspects of formative assessment they wished to develop in their practice and to identify a focal class with whom these strategies would be introduced in September 1999. Although there was no inherent structure in these plans, the teachers being free to explore whatever they wished, we did find that they could be organized under the broad headings shown in Table 3.1. In all, the twenty-four teachers included a total of 102 activities in their action plans – an average of just over four each – and while there was a small number of cases of teachers of the same subject at the same school adopting common plans, no other clustering of teachers was discernible.

Most of the teachers' plans contained reference to two or three important areas in their teaching where they were seeking to increase their use of formative assessment generally, followed by details of strategies that would be used to make this happen. In almost all cases, the plan was given in some detail,

Table 3.1 Frequencies of activities in the action plans of twenty-four teachers

Category	Activity	Frequency
Questioning	Teacher questioning	11
	Students writing questions	8
	Existing assessment: pre-tests	4
	Students asking questions	4
Feedback	Comment-only marking	6
	Existing assessment: re-timing	4
	Group work: test review	4
Sharing criteria with learners	Course work: marking criteria	5
	Course work: examples	4
	Start of lesson: making aim clear	4
	Start of lesson: setting targets	1
	End of lesson: teacher's review	1
	End of lesson: students' review	4
	Group work: explanation	2
	Involving classroom assessment	2
Self-assessment	Self-assessment: traffic lights	11
	Self-assessment: targets	5
	Group work: test review	6
	Self-assessment: other	7
	Student peer-assessment	5
	Group work: revision	1
General	Including parents	1
	Posters	1
	Presentations	1
Total		102

although many teachers used phrases whose meanings differed from teacher to teacher (even within the same school).

Practically every plan contained a reference to focusing on or improving the teacher's own questioning techniques, although not all of these gave details of the particular way in which they were going to do this. Many teachers also mentioned involving students more in setting questions, both for homework and for each other in class.

Using comment-only marking was specifically mentioned by six of the teachers: many others foresaw problems with this, given school policies on marking. Four teachers planned to bring forward end-of-module tests, thus providing time for feedback to achieve remediation.

Sharing the objectives of lessons or topics with students was mentioned by most of the teachers, through a variety of techniques. About half the plans included references to helping the students understand the marking criteria used for investigative or exploratory work, generally using exemplars from students from previous years. Exemplar material was also mentioned in other contexts.

Almost all the teachers mentioned some form of self-assessment in their plans, ranging from using red, amber or green 'traffic lights' to indicate the student's perception of the extent to which a topic or lesson had been understood, to strategies that encouraged self-assessment via targets that placed responsibility on students. Several teachers mentioned their conviction that group work provided important reinforcement for students, as well as providing the teacher with insights into their students' understanding of the work.

Observations of the classroom work of the teachers revealed that some activities specified in their plans did not appear to be implemented. However, while these amounted to about 10 per cent of the overall total, a number equivalent to about 60 per cent of that total appeared to have been added to the original plans during the period of implementation. The activities which showed the greatest increase in popularity were teacher questioning, students writing questions, students asking questions, comment-only marking and making aims clear at the start of a lesson.

The implementation of the action plans took place in the 1999/2000 school year, and so in the second phase of the work, which involved four further INSETs held between November 1999 and June 2000, the focus was on refining these action plans. Much of the work looked in finer detail at the various practices. One example of this was a discussion to which teachers brought samples of students' homework. By exchange of ideas and examples, this was to help meet the new challenge of framing comments on students' homework which could lead to improved learning, and of setting up procedures to ensure that these were followed up. Other issues explored included integrating learning goals with target setting and the use of personal diaries. A notable addition was a talk on learning theories given by one of us (D.W.) in response to requests from the teachers who had begun to realize that their new methods were forcing them to think afresh about their beliefs about learning, and about the integration of formative practices into their whole approach to teaching.

This last point illustrates an important aspect. The agenda of the INSETs was refined in the Steering Group sessions in the light of feedback both from the LEA staff who held their own discussions with their teachers, and by the King's staff who had observed lessons and talked with the teachers in their own schools. Thus as the work progressed, the INSETs came to reflect the agenda of the teachers, who gradually took over the initiative in the INSETs themselves, while our team were focused more on responding to needs and to capturing the new ideas that emerged, rather than on 'directing' the process.

For the third and final phase, involving five INSETs between September 2000 and July 2001, each school subject department was asked to fill any gaps, caused by the departure of teachers in the original group, with new colleagues, and in addition a new school was introduced because one of the original six appeared increasingly unable to release its teachers to come to the meetings. So one of the features in the 2000/2001 INSETs was the induction of these teachers. The experienced group played a major role in those parts of the meetings concerned with this process. This linked with more general explorations of dissemination within the schools and across the LEAs. The work with teachers of English, which commenced in October 2000, also provided a fresh input into discussions about the ways in which the new practices might be used, perhaps with adaptation, in all other school subjects.

The agendas of this last set of meetings included further exchanges of ideas on improving the quality of teachers' questioning, and a study of the links between formative and summative meetings. As part of this latter study, schools reported on such issues as the frequency of testing, the sources of the questions and mark schemes that they used, the records of student achievements that they kept, and the use of these records and other test data in reporting, in setting and in predicting GCSE grades.

The visits to schools

The other component of the intervention, the visits to the schools, provided an opportunity for project staff to observe lessons, to give feedback on these observations and to discuss with the teachers what they were doing and how this related to their efforts to put their action plans into practice. The interactions were not directive, but more like a holding up of a mirror to the teachers. Since project staff were frequently seen as 'experts' in either mathematics or science education, there was a tendency sometimes for teachers to invest questions from a member of the project team with a particular significance and, for this reason, these discussions were often more effective when science teachers were observed by mathematics specialists and vice versa.

We aimed for each teacher to be observed at least once each half-term, although releasing teachers to discuss their lessons either before or afterwards was occasionally a problem: schools that had guaranteed teacher release for this purpose at the beginning of the project were sometimes unable to provide for it. As mentioned above, these visits provided important information in helping to guide the future INSETs. They also yielded a body of qualitative data, as outlined below.

Work with teachers of English

This work was undertaken because we could not judge the extent to which the lessons learned in science and mathematics might be applicable in other subject areas. We chose to work with teachers of English for three reasons: the nature of the learning and the criteria of quality were very different from those in either science or mathematics, it was a core subject, and a leading expert in the subject (B.M.) was on the King's staff and interested in taking a lead in the work. The pattern of this work was broadly similar to that followed for the science and mathematics group. It was on a more restricted time-scale, but we were able to draw on the findings of the work in the other two subjects. Each school involved with the work in science and mathematics in 2000/2001 was asked to nominate two teachers, and this group of twelve took part in a set of five INSETs between October 2000 and July 2001. The qualitative information collected with these teachers was similar in character to that from their science and mathematics colleagues, but, given the constraints on resources and on time, it was not possible to collect quantitative data. Interesting differences between the different subjects were explored and the findings inform discussions throughout this book. The particular issue of differences between school subjects is discussed in Chapter 5.

Qualitative data

To meet the main aims of the project, the most important data were qualitative. These included:

- transcripts of interviews with individual teachers, conducted on each of three occasions – near the beginning, at the end of the first year and near the end of the second year;
- notes of lesson observations made at several stages;
- records of documents and observation notes from the INSET meetings;
- documents from the teachers setting out their action plans, with revisions of these;

- closing statements from each school about their plans to extend and disseminate the work;
- journals kept by many of the teachers;
- a closing statement by each teacher summing up his or her reflections on the experience of working to develop formative assessment;
- recordings of discussions with two groups of students about their perceptions of the changes in their classrooms: these are marginal, the main aim of the project being to focus on the collaborative development of teachers.

There are over 250 documents in total. Analysis of most of these forms the main basis for this book. More detailed analyses have been published or are in preparation for both professional and research journals. A full list is available on the King's website; details are provided at the end of the References.

Quantitative data

Although the collection and analysis of quantitative data is not the most important outcome of our project, it is nevertheless an important component. This is because the positive evidence of learning gains that it has produced can serve to reassure those who might be reluctant to take on new methods. In particular, they show that, far from putting at risk the test performances of their students and of their schools, they can improve these performances by better teaching.

The research design

The work of the project with teachers was designed to build on their professionalism rather than to impose a model of 'good formative assessment' . Each teacher was free to choose which class would be the focus for their action plan, and each was to follow both their normal curriculum and the normal testing and reporting requirements of their department and of their school – the project did not import any tests of its own. Thus, there was no possibility of conducting a standard research experiment.

It follows that the collection of empirical quantitative data about any learning gains had to be based on the normal assessment instruments used in each school. In many cases, these were the results for the 14-year-olds on national tests or the GCSE grades of 16-year-olds, but in many cases we made use of scores from school assessments, especially in science, where modular approaches meant that scores on end-of-module tests were available. For each teacher we negotiated a measure of the learning outcome of the focal class and a measure of input (i.e. of the achievement or 'ability' of that class), which could be compared with the 'input' of other classes.

To interpret the outcomes, we discussed the local circumstances in their school with each teacher and set up the best possible control group consistent with not disrupting the work of the school. In some cases, this was a parallel class taught by the same teacher in previous years (and in one case in the same year). In other cases, we used a parallel class taught by a different teacher and, failing that, a non-parallel class taught by the same or a different teacher. The input measures for both the focal and the control classes were provided in various ways – IQ scores (usually from the NFER's Cognitive Abilities Tests or CAT), school tests held at the end of the previous year or at the beginning of the action plan year, and both key stage 2 and key stage 3 tests. In almost all cases, calibration of the focal against the control groups was possible using one or more of these input measures, although in some cases they were measures of general ability (e.g. the CAT scores) while in others they were measures of achievement in the relevant subject (e.g. end-of-year 8 tests). To allow comparison of the results, raw differences between experimental and control groups were standardized to yield effect sizes, using the method described in Chapter 2.

Full details of the data and of the analysis used are given in Wiliam *et al.* (in press).

Results

Of the twenty-four teachers originally selected, reliable data were available for only nineteen. Four of these had decided to have two focal classes each, while for two more teachers there were two possible control groups. For reasons of completeness, all of these results were included, giving a total of 25 effect sizes in total.

Most of the effect sizes were around 0.2–0.3, with a mean of 0.34 and a median of 0.27; the reason for this difference was the biasing effect of three high values (over 1.0). Four of the values were negative. One was for a teacher who submitted two possible control classes: the comparison with the same teacher in a previous year gave a large positive effect (1.15), while comparison with another more experienced teacher with a parallel class in the same year gave the negative effect (–0.31). In a second case, the teacher was a newly qualified and female teacher starting in a boys' school and seen, from our observations, to be slowly overcoming initial difficulties with her classes. The only possible control comparison was with experienced male teachers in the same school. The other two negative results were for the two mathematics teachers at one school whose attendance at the in-service sessions had been irregular and whose engagement with formative assessment appeared, from the observations in visits, to be very limited. Thus there could be arguments

Table 3.2   Four ways in which teachers adopted formative assessment strategies

Experts	Formative assessment strategies embedded in and integrated with practice
Moving pioneers	Teachers who were successful with one or two key strategies, but having routinized these were looking for other ways to augment their practice
Static pioneers	Teachers who were successful with one or two key strategies and who had restricted themselves to these
Triallers	Teachers who had attempted strategies but had not embedded any strategies into their practice

for excluding all four, and if this were done the mean would rise to 0.46 and the median to 0.34. This would be reasonable if the aim were to estimate the effectiveness with those able to implement formative assessment effectively, but too optimistic if the aim were to evaluate the effectiveness in reality of an in-service programme.

To examine the relationship between a teacher's practice and the effect sizes, we classified teachers, according to their use of formative assessment strategies in their classrooms, into one of four groups, as shown in Table 3.2. These characterizations had emerged from our observations of each teacher's practice and were based on their use of key strategies during the main period of the project. There was no obvious trend, over these four groups, in terms of average effect size; however, the spread in the results across the more expert teachers was far smaller than the spread across the less expert. This result supports the view that the effects depend on the quality of the formative assessment work.

There was no difference in the mean effect size for groups of different ages, although it is worth pointing out that the year 11 focal groups – where the 'output' measure was the grade on the GCSE examination – all had positive effect sizes. There was no systematic variation in effect size with the input test performances of the focal classes.

Conclusion

By its very nature, the quantitative evidence provided here is difficult to interpret. The controls are not equally robust. In some cases, we have comparisons with the same teacher teaching a parallel class in previous years, which, in terms of the main question (i.e. has the intervention had an effect?), is probably the best form of control. In other cases, we have comparisons only with a different teacher teaching a parallel set, so it could be that in some cases a positive effect indicates only that the teacher participating in the project is a better teacher than the control. Furthermore, there was evidence of 'uncontrolled dissemination', whereby colleagues of teachers in the project were influenced by their reports to copy some of the new practices. In other cases, the control was another class (and sometimes a parallel class) taught by the same teacher, and while there are examples of positive effect sizes here, it is also reasonable to assume that the observed size of such effects would again be attenuated by 'uncontrolled dissemination', most of the teachers involved said that the effect of the project had spread beyond the focal class to all their classes. In some cases, the only controls available were the classes of different teachers teaching non-parallel classes, and given the prevalence of ability-grouping in mathematics and science and its effect on achievement (see Wiliam and Bartholomew 2001), disentangling the effect of our interventions from contextual factors was impossible.

Although a variety of measures were used as inputs and outputs, the fact that these were either national tests and examinations or assessments put in place by the school, gives us a degree of confidence that these measures have some validity in terms of what the teachers were trying to achieve.

Overall, the results cited above provide firm evidence that improving formative assessment does produce tangible benefits in terms of national assessments such as key stage 3 tests and GCSE examinations. The several complications cited above show that it is difficult to place a quantitative estimate on the size of the effect. However, even on the basis of the less optimistic of the median effect sizes reported above, it is likely that improvements equivalent to between one-quarter and one-half of a GCSE grade per student per subject are achievable. Although these improvements might sound small, if replicated across a whole school they would raise the performance of a school at the 25th percentile of achievement nationally into the upper half. At the very least, these data suggest that teachers do not have to choose between teaching well and getting good results.

4 Putting the ideas into practice

Four types of action

In this chapter, we describe teaching and learning practices that emerged from our project as both practical and rewarding. Some were introduced by us and others were invented by the project teachers; however, all were explored and transformed in the interplay between the King's team and the teachers and between the teachers themselves.

The King's, Medway, Oxfordshire Formative Assessment Project (KMO-FAP) set out to help teachers transform formative assessment ideas gleaned from research studies into working practice in the classroom. The ideas that motivated the teachers to change their practice were initially drawn from the four areas suggested in *Inside the Black Box* (Black and Wiliam 1998b):

- questioning;
- feedback;
- sharing criteria;
- self-assessment.

Over the course of the project, as teachers moved forward with their ideas they began developing and reshaping strategies. They found some ideas functioned better than others at bringing about changes in their classrooms which they found productive, and through their work on such experiences they were able to transform the implementation of formative assessment. One factor that influenced their decisions about what to try and what to develop was the context in which they found themselves. This was because they were having to make judgements about how formative assessment could be implemented within the constraints of their own assessment procedures and those of their school. These judgements had implications both for what they considered possible to attempt but also for the emphasis that they felt they should place on the different components of their assessment practices. By the end of the project, two of the original areas were still evident as distinct and specific areas in which to develop formative assessment practices; these were questioning and feedback. Both areas were pivotal in improving communication links between the teachers and their students about the assessment aspects of their work. Also, these areas had parts to play in many aspects of teaching, from face-to-face discussions to judging students' responses to feedback on written work. While the project revealed greater detail about how questioning and feedback played out in different classrooms, the principles underlying these two remained unscathed.

The other two, sharing criteria with learners and self-assessment, came to be understood differently. Sharing criteria with learners did have a role to play in formative assessment, but the ways in which this was approached meant that it served several other areas rather than standing alone alongside the other practices. It was subsumed into both the feedback and self-assessment categories: with feedback, criteria came to represent the framework from which teachers evolved appropriate comments to provide information to learners about achievement and for improvement; with self-assessment, it formed the framework that helped learners decide both how to make judgements about their own work and how to structure or detail their next piece of work.

Development of self-assessment was approached through the development of peer-assessment practices in the teachers' classrooms. Through the habits and skills of collaboration in peer-assessment, students were helped to develop the objectivity required for effective self-assessment, which gave them both a concept of what quality meant in a specific context and also the motivation to seek improvement.

As the project developed it became clear that the formative use of summative tests had an important part to play. Given the evidence of the harmful influence that narrow 'high-stakes' summative tests can have on teaching (Assessment Reform Group 2002), some have argued that formative and summative assessments are so different in purpose that they have to be kept apart. However, our teachers found it unrealistic to practise such separation and so sought to achieve a more positive relationship between the two, at least for those tests where the teacher has control over when and how they are used.

The outcome of these developments was that the project's main contribution was to take forward formative practice in four areas:

- questioning;
- feedback through marking;
- peer- and self-assessment by students;
- the formative use of summative tests.

The following sections look at the detail of how these four approaches were worked on and developed by the twenty-four science and mathematics teachers who began working on the KMOFAP project in February 1999, and the twelve teachers of English who began a year and a half later.

Questioning

Teachers recognize that questioning is an essential part of their practice. To focus our teachers on the difference that changes in their questioning might make to classroom interactions, we introduced them to the results of research on 'wait time' (Rowe 1974). This study in elementary science classes in the USA investigated classroom discourse and found that the mean time that teachers waited between asking a question and, if no answer was forthcoming, intervening again was only 0.9 seconds. When discussing this study, the KMOFAP teachers recognized that a wait time of less than one second prevented most students taking part in the classroom discourse. Such a short interval allowed insufficient time for them to think and then to formulate an answer. The teachers realized that they compromised by asking simple, closed questions where recall rather than thinking provides the answer. As a consequence, the dialogue was at a superficial level. Most of the teachers agreed that, in a bid to motivate the class and remind them of the previous lesson, they should start their lessons with a question-and-answer (Q&A) session of around 5 minutes, with the focus on remembering key words from previous work. This was substantiated by the classroom observations in the first few weeks of the project.

As one teacher described it :

> I'd become dissatisfied with the closed Q&A style that my unthinking teaching had fallen into, and I would frequently be lazy in my acceptance of right answers and sometimes even tacit complicity with a class to make sure none of us had to work too hard [. . .] They and I knew that if the Q&A wasn't going smoothly, I'd change the question, answer it myself or only seek answers from the 'brighter students'. There must have been times (still are?) where an outside observer would see my lessons as a small discussion group surrounded by many sleepy onlookers.
>
> I had always been wary of wrong answers. How do you respond to a child who willingly, enthusiastically puts their hand up, and every time has picked up the wrong end of the stick (or even a different stick altogether)? I want to encourage children to answer in class, but I need to challenge incorrect responses, so I'd usually end up with a lame 'That's an interesting way of looking at it', or 'Hmm, not quite what I had in mind'. No-one learnt anything from this exchange except the willing student, who gradually learnt to be less willing.
>
> (James, Two Bishops School)

Rowe (1974) went on to look at the effect of increasing the 'wait time'. She found the following changes associated with the classroom discourse:

- answers were longer;
- failure to respond decreased;
- responses were more confident;
- students challenged and/or improved the answers of other students;
- more alternative explanations were offered.

The teachers identified these changes in classroom discourse as desirable and tried over the following few weeks to increase the wait time in their lessons. In fact, to begin with the teachers were unable to increase their wait time above a few seconds and talked of 'unbearable silences' and concerns about 'kids switching off' or 'misbehaving' if the wait time was extended. Many teachers initially found it hard to increase their wait times – they had to break established habits and, as they changed, the expectations of their students were challenged:

> Increasing waiting time after asking questions proved difficult to start with – due to my habitual desire to 'add' something almost immediately after asking the original question. The pause after asking the question was sometimes 'painful'. It felt unnatural to have such a seemingly 'dead' period but I persevered. Given more thinking time, students seemed to realize that a more thoughtful answer was required. Now, after many months of changing my style of questioning I have noticed that most students will give an answer and an explanation (where necessary) without additional prompting.
>
> (Derek, Century Island School)

Other teachers also persevered and came to see value in their changed approach to classroom questioning:

> I chose a year 8 middle band group and really started to think about the type of questions I was asking – were they just instant one word answers, what were they testing – knowledge or understanding, was I giving the class enough time to answer the question, was I quickly accepting the correct answer, was I asking the girl to explain her answer, how was I dealing with the wrong answer? When I really stopped to think, I realized that I could make a very large difference to the girls' learning by using all their answers to govern the pace and content of the lesson.
>
> (Gwen, Waterford School)

To support the development of more effective question-and-answer sessions in the classroom, we introduced workshops on developing questioning skills in the second INSET at King's. In separate science and mathematics groups, the teachers considered a number of questions and considered how such questions might play out in the classroom discourse. They thought about the potential each question might have to promote thinking and discussion and predicted the types and varieties of answers that these questions might evoke from their classes. In this way, the teachers were able to identify questions that had formative potential. They were also helped to anticipate how they might refine and handle such questions in their classes and so were able to think ahead about where particular questions might lead. These issues also arose in later INSETs, where teachers shared and honed practice through peer support.

> Not until you analyse your own questioning do you realize how poor it can be. I found myself using questions to fill time and asking questions which required little thought from the students. When talking to students, particularly those who are experiencing difficulties, it is important to ask questions which get them thinking about the topic and will allow them to make the next step in the learning process. Simply directing them to the 'correct answer' is not useful.
>
> (Derek, Century Island School)

Discussions about particular questions helped the teachers gain confidence in using them in the classroom. By anticipating students' reaction to a question, and by hearing the views of other colleagues, teachers were helped to judge the suitability of questions and to modify them to fit the task in hand. So a question like 'Some people describe friction as the opposite of slipperiness. Do you agree or disagree?' was quickly changed to 'Some people describe friction as the opposite of slipperiness. What do you think?' Through such changes, students were encouraged to give thoughtful answers rather than simply to agree or disagree and then face the prospect of justifying their decision when they perhaps had reached that decision without sufficient thought as to why.

Other questions were considered useful in developing student reflection and promoting discussion. Examples of these would be:

> What do you think of Yagnesh's answer?
> What could we add to Suzie's answer?
> Dean said . . . and Monica thought . . . but how can we bring all these ideas together?

Focusing on what students said rather than on accepting an answer and moving on created enhanced opportunity for sustained discussion. The teachers thought it essential to encourage students to listen to and comment on answers being given by their peers, while at the same time ensuring that they feel comfortable in answering in the public domain of the classroom.

Increasing the wait time can lead to more students being involved in question-and-answer discussions and to an increase in the length of their replies. One particular way to increase participation is to ask students to brainstorm ideas, perhaps in pairs, for two to three minutes before the teacher asks for contributions. This allows students to voice their ideas, hear other ideas and articulate a considered answer rather than jumping in to utter the first thing that comes into their head in the hope that it is what the teacher is seeking. Overall, a consequence of such changes was that teachers learnt more about the pre-knowledge and understanding of their students, and about any gaps and misconceptions in that knowledge and understanding, so that their next moves could address the learners' real needs.

To exploit such changes, it is necessary to move away from the routine of limited factual questions and to re-focus attention on the quality and the different functions of classroom questions. An example is the use of a 'big question': an open question, or a problem-solving task, which can set the scene for a lesson, either by evoking a broad-ranging discussion or by prompting small group discussions, so involving many students. However, if this is to be productive, both the responses that the task might evoke and ways of following up these responses have to be anticipated. One teacher described an example of such a question:

> Nowadays, when we start a new unit, we start by looking at what we already know. This might be by having an in-depth question and answer session – with open-ended, challenging questions – such as, 'If plants need sunlight to make food, how come the biggest plants don't grow in deserts, where it's sunny all the time?' A *far better* lead in to the recall of photosynthesis than 'What is the equation for photosynthesis?' The former question allows all those students who don't even remember the word photosynthesis to begin formulating ideas and to be part of a discussion which gradually separates those who do remember and understand photosynthesis from those who don't.
>
> (Philip, Century Island School; teacher's emphasis)

The following two transcripts exemplify the change in the classroom culture of one of the science teachers as he worked on improving questioning as a formative tool in his classroom. The first transcript records an episode in September 1999, the second an episode in April 2000, some 8 months into the implementation phase of the project. Both transcripts form the start of a year seven (11- to 12-year-olds) lesson that moves onto a practical activity; however, the purpose of the teacher through his questioning differs between the two lessons and the experience for the learners is markedly different.

The first episode is an extract from a lesson about electricity:

Teacher: Right. I want everyone to concentrate now, because you need some information before you start today's experiment. Okay today we are going to find out about these . . .
Holds up an ammeter.
Teacher: Anyone know what we call these and where you might find one?
Starts to walk round and show groups the ammeter.
Two hands go up in the class.
Teacher: Look carefully. Where have you seen something like this? You might have seen something like it before. What is it involved with? It's got a special name . . .
Three more hands go up. The teacher selects one of these students.
Teacher: Yes . . . Jay?
Jay: In electricity, sir.
Teacher: That's right. You can use these in electric circuits. Anyone know what it is called? This word here helps. Can you read what it says? Carolyn?
Carolyn: Amps.
Teacher: And what is this instrument called that measures in amps ?
Pause of 2 seconds. No hands go up.
Teacher: No? No-one? Well, it's an ammeter because it measures in Amps? What's it called, Jamie?
Jamie: A clock, sir.
Teacher: You weren't listening Jamie. It might look like a clock but it is called an . . . ?
The teacher pauses and looks round class. Six hands shoot up.
Teacher: Richard?
Richard: An ampmeter sir.
Teacher: Nearly. Carolyn?
Carolyn: An ammeter.
Teacher: Thank you. What's it called Jamie?
Jamie: An ammeter.
Teacher: That's right. An ammeter. And where do we find these ammeters? Monica?
Monica shrugs her shoulders.
Six children have their hands raised.
Teacher: No idea. Tell her Rebecca.
Rebecca: In electric circuits.

Teacher: Good. I am starting to spot which of you are sleeping today. Are we with it now Monica?

Monica nods.

Teacher: Right. Now we are going to use these ammeters in our practical today and so gather round and I will show you how it works. Quietly please.

The students had been studying electric circuits for 2 weeks before this lesson and were familiar with the setting up of series and parallel circuits, but the teacher does not try to elicit their understanding in this extract. Instead, he engages in conversation with a few children to see if they can guess the two facts which he has in his head and which he wants them to grasp before they begin their experiment. The teacher's questioning is closed in nature. He wants to check that students know what things are called and where you find them. He plays a fast pace question-and-answer game, in which some students, like Carolyn and Rebecca, score points because they guess what the teacher wants them to say. Richard tries and nearly gets things right, while Jamie and Monica are highlighted for not paying attention.

The extract was discussed with the teacher as part of a discussion of the lesson by a visiting researcher. The teacher had felt uneasy during this part of the lesson because he thought more students would have known what an ammeter was and he also felt that several students, including Jamie and Monica, were not listening. He decided that he needed to work on the start to his lessons to involve more students in the question-and-answer sessions.

Over the next few months, this teacher worked on his concerns about wait time, about the small numbers of students who normally took part in whole class question-and-answer sessions, and about dealing with incorrect answers rather than ignoring them. These were addressed by radical changes in the rules and conventions of his classroom. This second extract, from a lesson about photosynthesis, was taken some 7 months later:

Teacher: We are going to look at the way plants feed today. I know you've done some work on this in your primary school and I am going to give you time to think that over and to tell your neighbour about what you know, or think you know already.

Students start looking at one another and a few whispers are heard.

Teacher: Hang on. Not yet. I want to give you something to think about.

The teacher produces two geranium plants from behind his desk. One is healthy and large and the other is quite spindly.

Teacher: Now when Mrs James potted up these two plants last spring, they were about the same size but look at them now. I think they might have been growing in different places in her prep room. I also think it's got something to do with the way that plants feed. So have a think, then talk to your partner. Why do you think these plants have grown differently?

The class erupts into loud discussion in pairs. The teacher goes over to sidebench and checks apparatus. After 4 minutes, the teacher returns to the front and stops the class discussion.

Teacher: Okay. Ideas?

About half the class put up their hands. Teacher waits for 3 seconds. A few more hands go up.

Teacher: Monica – your group? Pair?

Monica: That one's grown bigger because it was on the window. [*Pointing*]

Teacher: On the window? Mmm. What do you think Jamie?

Jamie: We thought that . . .

Teacher: You thought . . .?

Jamie: That the big 'un had eaten up more light.

Teacher: I think I know what Monica and Jamie are getting at, but can anyone put the ideas together? Window – Light – Plants?

Again about half the class put up their hands. The teacher chooses a child who has not put up his hand.

Teacher: Richard.

Richard: Err yes. We thought, me and Dean, that it had grown bigger because it was getting more food.

Some students stretch their hand up higher. The teacher points to Susan and nods.

Susan: No it grows where there's a lot of light and that's near the window.

Teacher: Mmmm. Richard and Dean think the plant's getting more food. Susan . . . and Stacey as well? Yes. Susan thinks it's because this plant is getting more light. What do others think? Tariq.

Tariq: It's the light cos its photosynthesis. Plants feed by photosynthesis.

The teacher writes photosynthesis on the board.

Teacher: Who else has heard this word before?

The teacher points to the board.

Almost all hands go up.

Teacher: Okay. Well can anyone put Plant, Light, Window and Photosynthesis together and tell me why these two plants have grown differently?

The teacher waits 12 seconds. Ten hands went up immediately he stopped speaking. Five more go up in the pause.

Teacher: Okay. Carolyn?

Carolyn: The plant . . . The big plant has been getting more light by the window and cos plants make their own food by photosynthesis, it's . . .

Jamie: Bigger.

Teacher: Thanks Jamie. What do others think about Carolyn's idea?
Many students nod.
Teacher: Yes its bigger because it has more light and can photosynthesize more. So Richard and Dean, how does your idea fit in with this?
Dean: It was wrong sir.
Richard: No it wasn't. We meant that. Photosynthesis. Plant food.
Dean: Yeah.
Teacher: So. Can you tell us your idea again but use the word photosynthesis as well this time?
Richard: Photosynthesis is what plants do when they feed and get bigger.
Teacher: Not bad. Remember that when we come to look at explaining the experiment that we are going to do today.

This extract shows a marked difference in the way that the teacher approaches questioning. He is no longer seeking terms and descriptions but rather trying to explore students' understanding. He creates opportunities for the students to exchange ideas, articulate their thoughts and to fashion answers in a supportive environment. Wait time is greatly extended and this encourages more students to participate and think of answers. The students' answers are longer and contain indications of their conceptual understanding rather than of their knowledge of names and terms.

The way that students participate in the classroom dialogue has changed. Jamie and Monica are much more involved in the question-and-answer session; this is particularly apparent when Jamie completes Carolyn's answer, indicating that he is both listening and thinking about what is being said. The answers suggest that students feel that their answers will be considered seriously by the teacher and any ambiguities or discrepancies pursued, such as when the teacher puts up Richard and Dean's answer along with Susan's answer for the class to consider. The aim is not for discrete right answers to be celebrated, but for a discussion of the ideas to be explored. The teacher no longer uses questioning in the way that he did in the electricity lesson, to support classroom management through revealing those students who fail to listen or refrain from taking part. Instead, questioning is used to elicit student understanding and promote shared learning in the photosynthesis lesson.

Questioning has been a continuing developmental theme throughout the project and has resulted in both teachers and their students changing their approaches in the classroom. The teachers report that they now spend more time preparing quality questions, have richer student involvement and use incorrect answers from both classwork and homework as discussion points to be taken up by the whole class. Questions are often devised to challenge common misconceptions, to create some conflict that requires discussion, or to explore ambiguity that needs clarification before an accepted answer can be formulated. Students are given time to think and sometimes to discuss their thoughts with peers, and then anyone might be asked to respond. Group responsibility is given a high profile in many of the classrooms so that mistakes can be shared and rectified and answers reached collectively and collaboratively. Students are therefore more ready to offer answers and to attempt difficult aspects, as they know that others will help them if they falter. So collaboration has emerged as the accepted community practice. There can also be effects on other parts of their work, as one teacher reported:

> There have been two very positive results from this approach. The most significant one is that because they have to explain their answers each time orally, this has carried through to their written work and now they set out their answers fully without being prompted. The second one is with a girl with a statement for being unable to talk or communicate with an adult. Having got used to the extra thinking time, she now offers answers orally and will now tentatively explain her answers.
>
> (Gwen, Waterford School)

One teacher summarized the overall effects of her efforts to improve the use of question-and-answer dialogue in the classroom as follows:

> *Questioning*
> My whole teaching style has become more interactive. Instead of showing how to find solutions, a question is asked and students given time to explore answers together. My year 8 target class is now well-used to this way of working. I find myself using this method more and more with other groups.
>
> *No hands*
> Unless specifically asked, students know not to put their hands up if they know the answer to a question. All students are expected to be able to answer at any time, even if it is an 'I don't know'.
>
> *Supportive climate*
> Students are comfortable with giving a wrong answer. They know that these can be as useful as correct ones. They are happy for other students to help explore their wrong answers further.
>
> (Nancy, Riverside School)

Like Nancy, many of the teachers in the project followed the suggestion of one of the group that it would be important to suppress the usual practice of having students put up their hands to volunteer to answer; they thereby discouraged the impulse to compete. Students' involvement in questioning took many forms: one of the ways to encourage this was to create opportunities for students to ask questions about pieces of work. The following example from one of the English classrooms illustrates this approach.

The students were eventually going to engage in a piece of autobiographical writing. The lesson entailed giving a year 7 mixed-ability class a brief passage called 'The Sick Boy', which the teacher had adapted, from Laurie Lee's novel *Cider With Rosie*, so that it was devoid of detail of any kind, giving the barest outline of events with little attention to the vocabulary or, to use the technical term, lexical density. The students were asked to annotate the text with any questions they would like to put to the author to make the text more interesting. The ideas were shared with partners as the teacher went around the class listening to the questions and prompting students to think of further ideas.

The questions were then collected and discussed by the class as a whole. The class were then read the actual extract from Laurie Lee's book and the students were asked to see how many of the questions were answered in the original text. This too was discussed. The lesson ended and was followed by another lesson immediately after lunch in which the questions were categorized as *factual*, such as 'what was someone's name?', or as *reactional empathetic*, such as 'how did this make the mother feel?' Lee's passage answered both types of question. These types of question were then used as the basis for the criteria by which the students' work was to be assessed. In other words, the teacher made explicit, as they began to write, that the features they had identified as helping to make a piece of writing more interesting would be the features by which their own work would be judged.

This lesson was early on in the sequence of lessons and demonstrates both how assessment informs planning and how students can become involved in the assessment process, albeit in a more subtle way. It is in effect an indication of how consideration of the criteria for success on the final piece of assessed work, and of ways to share these explicitly with the students, should form an important part of the planning process.

Questioning became an essential feature of the teachers' classrooms as questions were devised and used to promote thinking. This led to richer discourse, in which the teachers evoked a wealth of information from which to judge the current understanding of their students. More importantly, they had evidence on which to plan the next steps in learning so that the challenge and pace of lessons could be directed by formative assessment evidence rather than simply following some prescribed agenda. The task of improving questioning is a complex and gradual process, which involves the teacher in taking risks. More effort has to be spent in framing questions that are worth asking – that is, questions which explore issues that are critical to the development of students' understanding. Time has to be given to pursue students' ideas and rectify shortfalls. This involves creating or finding follow-up activities that are rich, in that they provide opportunities to ensure that meaningful interventions which extend the students' understanding can take place.

Overall, the main suggestions for action that have emerged from the teachers' innovations are:

- More effort has to be spent in framing questions that are worth asking; that is, questions which explore issues that are critical to the development of students' understanding.
- Wait time has to be increased to several seconds to allow students time to think and everyone should be expected to have an answer and to contribute to the discussion. Then all answers, right or wrong, can be used to develop understanding. The aim is thoughtful improvement rather than getting it right first time.
- Follow-up activities have to be rich, in that they provide opportunities to ensure that meaningful interventions that extend the students' understanding can take place.

Put simply, the only point of asking questions is to raise issues about which the teacher needs information or about which the students need to think.

Where such changes have been made, experience has shown that students become more active as participants and come to realize that learning may depend less on their capacity to spot the right answer and more on their readiness to express and discuss their own understanding. One teacher viewed the effects as follows:

> They have commented on the fact that they think I am more interested in the general way to get to an answer than a specific solution and when Clare [Lee] interviewed them they decided this was so that they could apply their understanding in a wider sense.
>
> (Belinda, Cornbury Estate School)

Feedback by marking

The second area in which the KMOFAP developed formative practices was feedback. An essential part of formative assessment is feedback to the learner, both to assess their current achievement and to indicate what the next steps in their learning trajectory should be. Just as the work on questioning brought out the importance of oral feedback, so for written feedback we introduced several relevant studies to the teachers. The one that created most discussion and influenced their work in this area was a study carried out by Ruth Butler and published in 1988.

Butler was interested in the type of feedback that students received on their written work. In a controlled experimental study, she set up three different ways of feedback to learners – marks, comments and a combination of marks and comments. The latter is the method by which most teachers provide feedback to their learners in the UK. The study showed that learning gains were greatest for the group given only comments, with the other two treatments showing no gains. Some of the teachers were shocked by these findings and initially could not envisage how marking by comments only would be possible in their schools. Other teachers in the group were goaded by their initial reaction to the research findings to try and make sense why and how comment-only marking might raise achievement. The study therefore created 'cognitive conflict' for some of the teachers, which led them to discuss and debate with colleagues to attempt to resolve their conflict. However, the study created cognitive inhibition for other teachers, who felt that their school situation prevented them even considering the proposed practice – feedback by comments without marks – as a possibility for them.

Those teachers who were able to discuss the possibilities of implementing comment-only marking were able to justify this practice from their classroom experiences in the following ways:

- students rarely read comments, preferring to compare marks with peers as their first reaction on getting work back;
- teachers rarely give students time in class to read comments that are written on work and probably few, if any, students return to consider these at home;
- often the comments are brief and/or not specific, for example 'Details?';
- the same written comments frequently recur in a student's book, implying that students do not take note of or act on the comments.

Such reflections on their practice, together with the impetus to seek change from the Butler study, encouraged the teachers to envisage how feedback might be used differently in their classrooms. This involved more than not giving a mark or grade. It involved finding the best way to communicate to the learners about what they had achieved and what they needed to work on next. It was also about engendering behaviours in the learners that would lead them to take action on the feedback and about providing a support system that fostered this approach. One teacher reported her experience as follows:

> My marking has developed from comments with targets and grades, which is the school policy, to comments and targets only. Students do work on targets and corrections more productively if no grades are given. Clare [Lee] observed on several occasions how little time

students spend reading my comments if there were grades given as well. My routine is now, in my target class, to: (i) not give grades, only comments; (ii) comments highlight what has been done well and what needs further work; (iii) the minimum follow-up work expected to be completed next time I mark the books.

(Nancy, Riverside School)

The way forward differed for each of the teachers and it seemed essential that each found practices that worked for them. So the honing of practice in individual classrooms was as important as the initial development of the idea. For some teachers, it was finding a new format for feedback that worked for them, while others focused on their classroom routines.

The project began guiding this change by first interviewing students in three of the schools and investigating their reaction to the way that their books were marked and the value they attached to the feedback comments that they received. The very clear messages from the students were that they wanted their teachers:

- to not use red pen because students felt that it ruined their work;
- to write legibly so that the comments could be read;
- to write statements that could be understood.

These messages were communicated to the teachers and, through discussion with project colleagues, they began to work on producing quality comments that could direct and motivate their students to improve their work. For example, a comment such as 'give more detail' may mean nothing to students if they cannot distinguish between relevant and irrelevant detail. Collaboration between the teachers in sharing examples of effective comments was helpful and experience led to more efficient fluency.

Most of the comments that we saw at the start of the project either stated a general evaluation, which indicated neither what had been achieved nor what steps to take next, or were geared to improving presentation or to merely completing work. Examples included: 'Good', 'Well done', 'Title?', 'Date?', 'Space out questions on the page', 'Rule off each piece of work', 'Use a pencil and a ruler for diagrams', 'Please finish' and 'Answer all the questions'.

As emphasized in the following extract, it was important to replace such comments by others that informed students about what they had achieved and what they needed to do next:

The important feature of this technique of course is the quality of the comment. A bland, non-helpful comment such as 'Good work Jaspaul, this is much neater and seems to show that you have tried hard' will not show any significant change in attainment because it says nothing about the individual's learning. There is no target and the student, although aware that the teacher is happy with them, could not be blamed for thinking that neatness is everything and that by keeping all of their work neat from now on, they will attain high grades. Students are not good at knowing how much they are learning, often because we as teachers do not tell them in an appropriate way.

(Dcrek, Century Island School)

Many of the teachers started each comment with the name of the individual student. This appeared to help them to identify the student and explain their needs at the outset.

James, you have provided clear diagrams and recognized which chemicals are elements and which are compounds. Can you give a general explanation of the difference between elements and compounds?

Susan, you have got the right idea here about trying to explain your rule. Think: does it apply to all triangles?

Richard, clear method, results table and graph, but what does this tell you about the relationship?

However, the names gradually disappeared and comments began to seek action as well as reflection on the piece of work:

Go back to your notes from the 29th September and look up where chlorophyll is and what it does.

You are fine with two −ve numbers but go back to your number line and work out +ve with −ve.

Well explained so far but add reasons why the Haber process uses these conditions.

Initial fears about how students might react to not receiving marks turned out to be unjustified. Students came to realize that the comments helped them in their future work:

At no time during the first 15 months of comment-only marking did any of the students ask me why they no longer received grades. It was as if they were not bothered by this omission. I found this amazing, particularly considering just how much emphasis students place on the grades and how little heed is taken of the comments generally. Only once, when the class was being observed by a member of the King's College team, did a student actually comment on the lack of grades. When asked by our visitor how she knew how well she was doing in science, the student clearly stated that the comments in her exercise book and those given verbally provide her with the information she needs. She was not prompted to say this!!!!

(Derek, Century Island School)

Also neither parents, senior management teams nor OFSTED inspectors have reacted adversely. Indeed, the provision of comments to students helps parents to focus on and support the students' learning rather than focus on uninformed efforts to interpret a mark or grade and/or to simply urge their child to work harder. We now believe that the effort that many teachers devote to marking work may be misdirected. A numerical mark does not tell a student how to improve their work, so an opportunity to enhance their learning has been lost.

In general, feedback given as rewards or grades enhances ego rather than task involvement – that is, it leads students to compare themselves with others and focus on their image and status rather than encourages them to think about the work itself and how they can improve it. Feedback by grades focuses students' attention on their 'ability' rather than on the importance of effort, damaging the self-esteem of low attainers. Feedback which focuses on what needs to be done can encourage all to believe that they can improve. Such feedback can enhance learning, both directly through the effort that can ensue and indirectly by supporting the motivation to invest such effort. A culture of success should be promoted where every student can make achievements by building on their previous performance, rather than by being compared with others. Such a culture is promoted by informing students about the strengths and weaknesses demonstrated in their work and by giving feedback about what their next steps should be. These points are discussed in greater depth in Chapter 5.

We have found a variety of ways of accommodating the new emphasis on comments. Some teachers cease to assign marks at all, some enter marks in record books but do not write them in the students' books, while others give marks only after a student has responded to their comments. A particularly valuable method is to devote some lesson time to redrafting one or two pieces of work, so that emphasis can be put on feedback for improvement within a supportive environment. This can change students' expectations about the purposes of classwork and homework.

Feedback by comments takes more time than giving marks, and the teachers found ways of creating adequate time gaps to formulate effective comments which could give students ideas and confidence for improving their work. Once again, the way forward was based on discussions by the group of teachers as a whole and then practices were modified within each teacher's classroom. One teacher dealt with the challenge as follows:

> The whole faculty moved to a comment-only assessment policy in September in the light of the KMOFAP work. I am not aware of a single parent expressing concern over a lack of grades/levels/marks. I am marking less frequently, and often not particularly well, but I mark well once every 3 weeks at present. In theory I would like to do this more, but until we halve class sizes or contact time, or give up having a life, I don't see this as likely. My aim is to feel less guilty about marking less rather than to try to mark more!
>
> (James, Two Bishops School)

Like James, several teachers spent more time on certain pieces of work to ensure that they could provide good feedback and, to make time for this, did not mark some pieces, marked only a third of their students' books each week or involved the students in checking straightforward tasks. New procedures were also needed to ensure that both teachers and students were aware of how problems were being tackled and what the students' targets were in future pieces of work. One example was:

> After the first INSET I was keen to try out a different way of marking books to give pupils a more constructive feedback. I was keen to try and have a more easy method of monitoring pupils' response to my comments without having to trawl through their books each time to find out if they'd addressed my comments. I implemented a comment sheet at the back of my year 8 class's books. It was A4 in size and the left-hand side is for my comments and the right-hand side is for the pupils to demonstrate by a reference to the page in their books where I can find the evidence to say whether they have done the work [. . .] The comments have become more meaningful as the time has gone on and the books still only take me one hour to mark.
>
> (Sian, Cornbury Estate School)

One reason why comment-only marking took time to develop in the early stages of the project was that the teachers had to develop and hone better ways of writing comments. Being aware of Kluger and DeNisi's (1996) research review, which showed that feedback only leads to learning gains when it included guidance about how to improve (see Chapter 2), the teachers knew that they had to be thoughtful and careful about how they wrote their comments. So devising the wording for comment-only marking took time and effort for each teacher. The result was that teachers focused in their comments on trying to encourage and direct their students to improve their work, with the emphasis on mastery of learning rather than on the grading of performance.

As they tried to create useful feedback comments, many of the project teachers realized that they needed to reassess the work that they had asked students to undertake. They found that some tasks were useful in revealing students' understandings and misunderstandings, but that others focused mainly on conveying information. So some activities were eliminated, others modified and new and better tasks actively sought. Time was also taken by the teachers in reflecting on schemes of work for specific topics and recognizing those activities in which there was opportunity to create a range of good comments. These activities tended to be quite challenging and, in some topics, the teachers realized that such activities had been either sparse or absent. This meant that teachers had to find some alternative activities and these took time to plan and prepare. A further factor that took time was finding appropriate follow-on activities in which students could make another attempt at demonstrating the improvements that the teacher had suggested in their feedback comments. While in some cases this was unnecessary because students redrafted and improved the original piece of work, there were occasions when teachers spent time and effort seeking or creating new activities to help students to take action for improvement.

Gradually, both teachers and learners became more familiar and more skilful in dealing with comment-only marking and, as they did so, the classroom culture began to change. They all came to understand that it was worthwhile putting in the effort to work with feedback by comments because they could sense that learning was improving. The comments provided the vehicle for personal dialogue with each learner about his or her work to which the learner could respond. However, the development was more important than that because the teachers came to realize that they needed to create learning environments that supported and fostered good learning behaviours in their students and again they looked to research for ideas and direction.

Although our teachers had to piece together the various features of their classroom environment, a 1990 study of learning major scales in music by 12-year-olds (Boulet *et al.* 1990) provoked ideas, discussion and reflection. In this research, one experimental group of students were given written praise, a list of weaknesses and a work-plan, while a second experimental group were given oral feedback, with guidance about the nature of their errors and a chance to correct them. A third group acted as a control and were given no feedback. The results showed that the second experimental group did better at learning their scales. Although the conclusions from this study are ambiguous because two variables were changed together between the two experiments, it does provides some evidence of what an effective learning environment ought to include, and it has been found to provide a fruitful basis for discussion. When teachers come to discuss the outcome, they begin to surmise what the two experimental classrooms might be like, using their own experiences as teachers and learners to imagine the contrast between the learning situations that the two experimental groups set up. While some teachers might focus on one specific variable having a causal effect, others might use the variables to explain the complexities and nuances of a classroom environment in which the purpose is to improve learning. Thus the issues behind these ideas are brought to the fore and teachers seek both the means and the reassurance to foster good learning environments.

Overall, the main ideas for improvement of learning through students' written work were :

- Written tasks, alongside oral questioning, should encourage students to develop and show understanding of the key features of what they have learnt.
- Comments should identify what has been done well and what still needs improvement, and give guidance on how to make that improvement.
- Opportunities for students to follow up comments should be planned as part of the overall learning process.

Peer- and self-assessment

As explained in Chapter 2, the starting point here was the work of Sadler (1989). It is very difficult for students to achieve a learning goal unless they understand that goal and can assess what they need to do to reach it. So self-assessment is essential to learning. Many who have tried to develop self-assessment skills have found that the first and most difficult task is to get students to think of their work in terms of a set of goals. Insofar as they do, students begin to develop an overview of that work so that it becomes possible for them to manage and control it for themselves. One teacher identified the key features as follows:

> I have thought carefully about pupils taking *ownership* of their own learning. I have now thought more about letting pupils know what the intention of the lesson is and what they need to do to *achieve it*. This way they have to think what they know and take more *responsibility* for their own learning.
>
> (Angela, Cornbury Estate School; teacher's emphasis)

At the start of the project, initial attempts at self-assessment and target-setting by students were unsuccessful. The teachers saw that the source of the problem was that their students lacked the necessary skills both to judge specific problems in understanding and to set realistic targets to remedy problems within reasonable time frames. However, those teachers who introduced feedback by comments, and thereby created the classroom environments where students worked together on understanding teacher comments about their work, were providing the training that students needed to judge their own learning and to begin to take action to improve.

In practice, peer-assessment turns out to be an important complement and may even be a prior requirement for self-assessment. Peer-assessment is uniquely valuable for several reasons. One is that prospect of such assessment has been found to improve the motivation of students to work more carefully:

> As well as assessing and marking (through discussion and clear guidance) their own work, they also assess and mark the work of others. This they do in a very mature and sensible way and this has proved to be a very worthwhile experiment. The students know that homework will be checked by themselves or another girl in the class at the start of the next lesson. This has led to a well-established routine and only on extremely rare occasions have students failed to complete the work set. They take pride in clear and well-presented work that one of their peers may be asked to mark. Any disagreement about the answer is thoroughly and openly discussed until agreement is reached.
>
> (Alice, Waterford School)

A second reason is that the interchange in peer discussions is in language that students themselves would naturally use. Their communication with one another can use shared language forms and can provide tenable models, so that the achievements of some can convey the meaning and value of the exercise to others still struggling. An additional factor is that students often accept, from one another, criticisms of their work that they would not take seriously if made by their teacher.

A third advantage is that feedback from a group to a teacher can command more attention than that of an individual and so peer-assessment helps strengthen the student voice and improves communication between students and their teacher about their learning. This can also make the teacher's task more maneagable, for it helps the learners to recognize their own learning needs and to inform the teacher about these needs. A further advantage is that when students are busy, involved in peer assessment in the classroom, the teacher can be free to observe and reflect on what is happening and to frame helpful interventions:

> We regularly do peer marking – I find this very helpful indeed. A lot of misconceptions come to the fore and we then discuss these as we are

going over the homework. I then go over the peer marking and talk to students individually as I go round the room.

(Rose, Brownfields School)

In general, students' learning can be enriched by marking their own or one another's work, whether this be classswork, homework, test scripts or presentations to the class. Students learn by taking the roles of teachers and examiners of others.

One simple and effective idea is for students to use 'traffic light' icons, labelling their work green, amber or red according to whether they think they have good, partial or little understanding. These labels serve as a simple means of communication of students' confidence in their work and so act as a form of self-assessment. Students may then be asked to justify their judgements in a peer-group, so linking peer- and self-assessment. This linkage can help in the development of the skills and the detachment needed for effective self-assessment. So it appears that peer-assessment is an important factor in helping students develop the essential skills that they require for self-assessment.

Teachers developed a variety of classroom strategies to explore these habits and skills. The following teacher used them as part of work on 'investigations' in mathematics.

Using formative assessment to aid investigational work has been very successful and I intend to use it with year 10 and 11 in the future for their course work. I gave my year 9 group an easy investigation on area and they went away and did this. On the lesson it was due in, I got them to mark their peers' investigational work straight from the actual NC [national curriculum] levels. I was really surprised with the attention they paid to the work and to the levels. They also gave excellent reasons for giving that person's work the level they did. The work was swapped back and the pupil then had to produce targets for their own work. There was a class discussion at the end of the lesson on their targets and they then had to go away and rewrite the investigational work. This process was repeated one more time, bar the rewrite. The results were excellent and most had improved by two grades. I found when marking the work that some had not quite got the gist of it, but that will come with repetition of the task in the future.

(Lily, Brownfields School)

Another approach is to ask students first to 'traffic-light' a piece of work and then to indicate by a show of hands whether they put green, amber or red; the teacher can then pair up the greens and ambers to deal with problems between them, while the red students can be helped as a group to deal with their deeper problems. This is instant differentiation but the recognition of the learning needs has been done by the students, allowing the teacher to focus on steering the remedial action. Because the response to their needs is immediate, students begin to realize that revealing their problems is worthwhile, as the focus of the teaching is to improve learning rather than to compare one student with another.

Peer- and self-assessment helped the project teachers to make the criteria for evaluating any learning achievements transparent to students, so enabling them to develop a clear overview both of the aims of their work and of what it meant to complete it successfully. Such criteria were sometimes abstract and so concrete examples were used in modelling exercises to develop understanding. Suitable models were often drawn from other students' work, either from previous years or from the class itself, although these pieces were sometimes modified by the teacher to emphasize particular aspects or the lack of evidence for a specific criterion.

However, peer- and self-assessment will only thrive if teachers help their students, particularly the low-attainers, to develop the skill. As one teacher found, this can take time and practice:

> The kids are not skilled in what I am trying to get them to do. I think the process is more effective long term. If you invest time in it, it will pay off big dividends, this process of getting the students to be more independent in the way that they learn and taking the responsibility themselves.
>
> (Tom, Riverside School)

For such peer-group work to succeed, many students will need guidance about how to behave in groups – for example, in listening to one another and taking turns – and once again this takes time and care if it is to succeed in the classroom. Students should be taught the habits and skills of collaboration in peer-assessment, both because these are of intrinsic value and because peer-assessment can help develop the objectivity required for effective self-assessment.

Our experience of work on this theme leads to the following recommendations for improving classroom practice:

- The criteria for evaluating any learning achievements must be made transparent to students to enable them to have a clear overview both of the aims of their work and of what it means to complete it successfully. Such criteria may well be abstract – concrete examples should be used in modelling exercises to develop understanding.
- Students should be taught the habits and skills of collaboration in peer-assessment, both because these are of intrinsic value and because

peer-assessment can help develop the objectivity required for effective self-assessment.

- Students should be encouraged to bear in mind the aims of their work
  and to assess their own progress to meet these aims as they proceed.
  They will then be able to guide their own work and so become
  independent learners.

The main point here is that peer- and self-assessment make unique contributions to the development of students' learning – they secure aims that cannot
be achieved in any other way.

The formative use of summative tests

At the start of the project, we tried to encourage teachers to steer clear of
summative assessment as they developed their formative work, because of
the negative influences of summative pressures on formative practice. The
teachers could not accept such advice because their reality was that formative assessment had to work alongside summative assessment. They tried
instead to work out effective strategies for using formative approaches to
summative tests. These involved both using formative strategies to aid preparation for summative tests, and using them as a means of identifying learning targets from the detailed evidence that summative test questions could
produce.

In a first innovation, the teachers used formative practices to support revision and develop more effective reviewing strategies, for example in tackling
the following problem:

> When I asked them what preparation they did before the test they
> would often say, 'Revise, Sir'. They did not mention any of the review-
> ing strategies we had discussed in class. When questioned more
> closely, it was clear that many spent their time using very passive
> revision techniques. They would read over their work doing very little
> in the way of active revision or reviewing of their work. They were not
> transferring the active learning strategies we were using in class to
> work they did at home.
>
> (Tom, Riverside School)

The overall finding was that to change this situation, students should be
engaged in a reflective review of the work they have done to enable them to
plan their revision effectively. One way is for students to 'traffic-light' a list of
key words, or a number of questions from a test paper of the topics on which
the test will be set. The point of this is to stimulate the students to reflect on

where they feel their learning is secure, which they mark green, and where they need to concentrate their efforts, which they mark amber or red. These traffic lights then form the basis of a revision plan. Students can be asked to identify questions on past examination papers that test their red areas and then work with books and in peer groups to ensure they can answer those questions successfully. This helps students structure their revision so that they work on their areas of weakness rather than simply reviewing what they already know. One teacher described a way of using peer group work that could help with revision:

> One technique has been to put the students into small groups and give each student a small part of the unit to explain to their colleagues. They are given a few minutes preparation time, a few hints and use of their exercise books. Then each student explains their chosen subject to the rest of their group. Students are quick to point out such things as, 'I thought that the examples you chose were very good as they were not ones in our books. I don't think I would have thought of those'. Or, 'I expected you to mention particles more when you were explaining the difference between liquids and gases'. These sessions have proven invaluable, not only to me, in being able to discover the level of understanding of some students, but to the students too.
>
> (Philip, Century Island School)

A second innovation was suggested by research studies (King 1992; Foos *et al.* 1994) that have shown that students trained to prepare for examinations by generating and then answering their own questions outperform comparable groups who prepared in conventional ways. When students are encouraged to set questions and mark answers, this can help them both to understand the assessment process and to focus further efforts for improvement. Preparation of test questions calls for, and so develops, an overview of the topic:

> More significantly, pupils' setting of their own questions has proved to be a stimulating and productive means of rounding off topics and revising their work. Answering other people's questions and discussing solutions with the whole class is a very effective way of concentrating on topics that need to be revised rather than spending time on what is already known. Students have had to think about what makes a good question for a test and in doing so need to have a clear understanding of the subject material. As a development of this, the best questions have been used for class tests. In this way, the students can see that their work is valued and I can make an assessment of the progress made in these areas. When going over the test, good use can

be made of group work and discussions between students concentrating on specific areas of concern.

(Angela, Cornbury Estate School)

A third innovation was to use the aftermath of tests as an opportunity for formative work. Teachers might, for example, look to see which questions were poorly done by most students and concentrate on rectifying the learning associated with those, rather than simply working through a mark scheme where the focus is on claiming a few extra marks rather than on focusing on learning. Peer marking of test papers can also be helpful, as with normal written work, and is particularly useful if students are required first to formulate a mark scheme, an exercise which focuses attention on criteria of quality relevant to their productions, as this teacher describes:

> Now, the papers are returned, and students work in small groups to agree on answers – in effect coming up with their own mark scheme. This works best in practice, I have found, if only a few questions are tackled at a time, then the class share information, and make sure that they are in agreement with the official mark scheme, then on to the next few questions. Initially, this tended towards, '*I must be wrong because I'm the only one who has that answer*'. And that is still a problem with lower ability students, who lack confidence. Quickly, however, the middle ability and more able pupil is able to realize that the best answer is not necessarily the majority one, but the one that can be best justified.
>
> (Philip, Century Island School; teacher's emphasis)

As with the test review, after peer marking, teachers can reserve their time for discussion of the questions that give particular difficulty; those problems encountered by only a minority can be tackled by peer tutoring.

As with all forms of their written work, students can be encouraged through peer- and self-assessment to apply criteria to help them understand how their test answers might be improved. This may include providing them with opportunities to discuss and clarify how criteria play out in a piece of work, to recognize which areas need to be improved to create a quality piece of work, and then to be given the opportunity to re-work examination answers in class.

These developments challenge the view frequently expressed that formative and summative assessments are so different in their purpose that they have to be kept apart, views which are supported by experience of the harmful influence that narrow 'high-stakes' summative tests can have on teaching. However, it is unrealistic to expect teachers and students to practise such separation, so the challenge is to achieve a more positive relationship between the two. This section has set out ways in which this can be done: they can all be used for tests where teachers have control over the setting and the marking, but their application may be more limited for tests where the teacher has little or no control.

We must add a caveat to this message about summative tests and their formative use. The project schools felt constrained to make frequent use of questions from key stage 3 and GCSE examinations to familiarize their students with these. This, at times, limited the formative dimension, as the focus moved from developing understanding to 'teaching to the test'. More generally, the pressures exerted by current external testing and assessment requirements are not fully consistent with good formative practices. Although most of our teachers were able to remove the conflict between formative and summative assessment for some parts of their schemes of work, frequent summative testing dulled the message about the means to improve, replacing it with information about successes or failures. While our work with schools showed evidence of a lack of synergy across this internal/external interface, the study of this problem lay outside the scope of this project.

Overall, the main possibilities for improving classroom practice are as follows:

- Students should be engaged in a reflective review of the work they have done to enable them to plan their revision effectively.
- Students should be encouraged to set questions and mark answers to help them, both to understand the assessment process and to focus further efforts for improvement.
- Students should be encouraged through peer- and self-assessment to apply criteria to help them understand how their work might be improved. This may include providing opportunities for them to re-work examination answers in class.

The overall message is that summative tests should be, and should be seen to be, a positive part of the learning process. Such tests should be used to chart learning occasionally rather than to dominate the assessment picture for both teachers and students. Active involvement of students in the test process can help them to see that they can be beneficiaries rather than victims of testing, because tests can help them improve their learning:

> After each end-of-term test, the class is grouped now to learn from each other. Clare Lee has interviewed them on this experience and they are very positive about the effects. Some of their comments show that they are starting to value the learning process more highly and they appreciate the fact that misunderstandings are given time to be resolved, either in groups or by me. They feel that the pressure to

succeed in tests is being replaced by the need to understand the work
that has been covered and the test is just an assessment along the way
of what needs more work and what seems to be fine.

(Belinda, Cornbury Estate School)

Implications

The new practices described in this chapter are far more rich and more extensive than those we were able to suggest at the outset of the project on the basis
of the research literature. All of them involve teachers in reflecting on their
current practice and involve changes in the way that they work with their
students and with the curriculum. This vividly demonstrates that, with support, teachers can transform research results into new and effective practices.

We do not wish to imply that the set of four activities is a closed and
complete set – that is, there may be other activities that could, if developed
with formative principles in mind, further enrich formative work. For
example, we did not explore concept maps, but only because in our original
survey we did not find any research on their formative use. Two of the project
teachers tried to use them to explore student's understanding but found they
took too much time and yielded information that was not detailed enough to
capture important problems. This indicates that further development work is
needed, taking up, for example, the implication from research (Ruiz-Primo *et
al.* 2001) that students' labelling and explanation of the links between the
concept nodes might yield the most useful information. Similarly, other
teachers were keen to explore target-setting in a formative context, but found
in the current school practice that the targets were on too coarse a scale and
could not be understood by many students. When they were made more
detailed and fine-grained, then the task of ensuring that the learner understood required the use of peer- and self-assessment approaches and the exercise
merged into the work in our four main activities. Our general conclusion is
that any additional activity will probably need careful study and development
if it is to add power to the four described in this chapter.

Our work with the KMOFAP teachers has raised more fundamental issues
about teaching, learning and assessment, which we discuss in Chapter 5. The
personal processes of change for teachers are then considered in more detail in
Chapter 6. That this is not a simple process is obvious and the trajectory for
individual teachers, departments and schools will differ because starting
points will vary, as will the beliefs, wishes and efforts of those embarking on
such changes. For such practice to be developed and then sustained requires
that teachers be supported at a variety of levels: we look at this in Chapter 7.

5 Looking at practice more deeply

In Chapter 4, we saw how the teachers put formative assessment into practice in their own classrooms. In this and the following chapter, we look a little more deeply at what happened as a result and reflect on some of the broader issues raised by our experiences. Here we look at the relationship between subject knowledge and learning needs, the differences between subjects, how the work of the teachers impacted on the attitudes and beliefs of their students, and links with research into learning. In Chapter 6, we look in detail at some of the changes in the teachers involved with the project.

Subject knowledge and learning needs

As the teachers in the project became more thoughtful about the feedback they were giving students, they became increasingly dissatisfied with their practice. In particular, when the mathematics and science teachers were marking their students' work, they often found that although they could tell the students what was right and what was not, they found it extremely difficult, if not impossible, to offer advice to the students as to how to improve. The reason for this was, of course, that the tasks that had been set had not been designed for this purpose. The teacher knew whether the students had learnt the material successfully or not, but in marking the students' work they learnt nothing about the reasons for any difficulty, or what they might do about it. In other words, the tasks were not rich enough to provide evidence for the teacher, in that seeing the students' responses did not allow them to tap into students' understanding. It became clear that good feedback started with good planning – unless the tasks were specifically designed and framed so as to support feedback, it was highly unlikely that they would do so.

Designing good tasks, activities or questions requires that teachers have good subject knowledge, but this is not the kind of abstract subject knowledge that is developed through advanced study of a subject. Advanced study often produces individuals who partially understand a great deal of advanced material, while effective teachers need to understand thoroughly the basic material (Askew *et al*. 1997). Moreover, if teachers are to design good tasks, and respond helpfully to the students' efforts, then thorough and profound subject knowledge is not enough. Teachers also need good models of how students are thinking about a particular topic. We should, therefore, not have been as surprised as we were when, as noted in Chapter 3, during the early INSET sessions the teachers asked us to organize a session on the psychology of learning. They had realized that they needed better models of how their students thought if they were to make sense of their responses to tasks, activities and questions, and to respond in ways that supported learning. In other words, they needed to develop not their abstract subject knowledge, but what Shulman (1986) calls 'pedagogical content knowledge' – knowing which aspects of a subject cause students particular difficulties, and knowing the metaphors, contexts and analogies that students find helpful.

As the teachers came to listen more attentively to the students' responses, they began to appreciate more fully that learning was not a process of passive reception of knowledge, but one in which the learners were active in creating their own understandings. It became clear that, no matter what the pressure to achieve good test and examination scores, learning cannot be done *for* the student; it has to be done *by* the student. The teacher's role is to 'scaffold' this process – that is, to provide a framework of appropriate targets and to give support in the task of attaining them. But it also became increasingly clear that the teachers also needed to train their students to take responsibility for their own learning and assessment (for more on this, see Chapter 6).

The changes in the KMOFAP classrooms over the life of the project were striking. The teachers gradually developed learning environments that focused on improvement and this was achieved through evolving and supporting collaborative learning within their classrooms. Although the journeys to establishing collaborative learning differed, there were some common themes. As we saw in Chapter 4, the teachers sought the student voice and eventually participation in deciding the pace and direction that teaching and learning should take. The effect of the project might be summarized as making the students' voices louder and making the teachers' hearing better.

Throughout the 18 months of the project, all teachers at some stage worked on 'wait time', improving the quality of their questions and implementing richer dialogues in their classrooms. Approximately half of the teachers started with this strategy as one of their priorities but, one by one, the other teachers came to see the improvement of questioning as a way forward with their formative practice. They came to see that the way that classroom questioning sessions were conducted had profound effects upon the culture of their classroom. It shifted the emphasis from teaching about the subject to attending to students' needs. But more than this, it helped the students to become more active in the learning process, as well as developing a reliance on each other rather than solely on the teacher. The learners began to see that collaboration had rewards and uses that competition did not (see the section below on 'Attitudes and beliefs').

The transcripts for the photosynthesis and electricity lessons in Chapter 4 bear this out. In the photosynthesis lesson, the teacher arranged for the students to discuss his question in pairs before answering in the public domain of the classroom. Here, everyone had to say what they thought the answer might be and, on hearing their partner's response (whether it was agreement, a challenge to their ideas or an alternative approach), they either consolidated or modified their original ideas. Then, because the teacher encouraged students to comment on what others had answered, there was further opportunity for each learner to evaluate and, if necessary, alter their ideas. In this way, the answers of the students helped individual learners construct their knowledge, and this was structured or 'scaffolded' (Wood *et al.* 1976) by the questioning and facilitatory skills of the teacher.

This process of making one's thinking explicit through talking is important for two reasons. As noted above, it allows teachers some access into the student's thinking, so they can intervene to address misconceptions or to promote further learning. This is nicely illustrated by a science lesson at Century Island School in which Philip was teaching a year 7 class about light. Through the use of open-ended and higher-order questions, he discovered that the class already knew from their primary schooling all the content he had planned for the lesson, but their answers also revealed that what the students lacked were the appropriate connections between the components of their existing knowledge. Once aware of this, he was able to change the focus of the lesson away from teaching the content he had originally planned and towards the relationships within the content that the students already knew.

As well as helping the teacher, getting students to make their thinking explicit is also important for the learner because it actually causes learning. It is tempting to view the process of questioning as 'probing' to determine whether the requisite knowledge is stored somewhere in a student's head, and this may well be a good model of what is going on when the teacher asks 'lower-order' questions, such as those that require merely recall of facts. However, when the teacher asks 'higher-order' questions – questions that explore understanding and require thinking – the student is not just recalling knowledge but building it. This is why allowing students enough time in questioning sessions is important.

In this context, it is worth noting that the research on wait-time identifies two sorts of 'wait time': there is the gap between the teacher finishing the question and the start of the student's response, and there is also the gap between the end of the student's response and the teacher's response to the student's response. Both are important. The first allows students time to mar-shal their thoughts and to begin to assemble an answer, but the second wait time, allowing students time to extend, elaborate or just to continue their answer, also improves learning.

Because the opportunities for students to articulate their thoughts in a whole-class session are limited, many of the teachers began to appreciate the usefulness of small group work, which created more opportunities for students to talk about their work. Students articulated their own understanding and the contributions of others in the group were 'scaffolded', but here the scaffolding was provided by peers.

One concern voiced by some of the teachers at this stage was that too much group work might 'hold back' the higher-attaining students, which was no doubt exacerbated by the concern of many school inspectors with the extent to which the teacher had provided for 'differentiation' in their lessons. However, the research on students working in small groups shows that those who give help to others generally benefit most (see Askew and Wiliam 1995). This is not surprising. Almost every teacher discovers that they only really understand something when they have to teach it, and by being forced to articulate one's understanding, high-attainers are forced to make richer and more profound links to their existing knowledge, thus strengthening long-term retention.

Another key change in the KMOFAP classrooms was that it became clear that it was essential for students to come to understand what counted as good work, as noted by Royce Sadler (1989). This, too, was taken forward in small groups, through students' assessment of their own and their peers' work.

Teachers tackled peer- and self-assessment in a number of ways. In some instances they asked the students to create their own criteria, while in others they used the criteria supplied by the examination boards. Some then asked the students to simplify the language, or provided simplified versions them-selves, while others felt that it was useful for the students to grapple with the 'official' language of the criteria and negotiate their meaning. However, it is also important to note that students were able to engage in effective self- and peer-assessment not just in mathematics, where a precise marking scheme could be given to the students, but also when specific criteria were not avail-able, as the following extracts from lessons illustrate.

The first example comes from a mixed-ability year 9 class taught by Piers at Two Bishops School. All the students had just completed a 'mock' (trial) key stage 3 test. Piers had read through all the scripts and identified several questions on which all the students had done badly in the reading paper. He handed the papers back unmarked and asked them to think about a mark scheme for 'levelling' these papers. He then asked for contributions from the class to create a class mark scheme. After some discussion, they agreed on the following:

- *Level 3*:   Good punctuation and spelling and be able to answer the required question.
- *Level 4*:   All of the above, good use of PEE (Point, Evidence, Explanation), good length answer.
- *Level 5*:   All of the above, good use of PEE , well explained answer.
- *Level 6*:   All of the above, good use of language and time.
- *Level 7*:   All of the above, couldn't be better.

Piers then identified a particular question from the test and asked them to identify in pairs what they would need to change in a response to go up one level. To this extent, the students were involved in both peer- and self-assessment, or in self-assessment with the aid of a peer in discussion. In these discussions, the following comments were made:

> I think in our comments we could have explained more.
> They used generally formal language except for 'freaked out'.
> We didn't use enough quotes; we could have had one per paragraph.

The activity was then followed by a detailed re-working of one of the questions which the students then re-levelled.

Although the use of national curriculum levels may provide a starting point, it is important to note that an over-emphasis on the levels may be counterproductive. The ultimate aim of peer- and self-assessment is not that students can give each other levels and grades – these are merely means to an end. Too much emphasis on getting students to use national curriculum levels and GCSE grades can divert attention away from the real purpose – the identification of learning needs and the means of improvement.

The second lesson is a top-set year 11 English lesson taught by Mary at Riverside School working on preparation for timed examination essay answers. The class spent the first half of the lesson on a timed essay on the section of the syllabus on 'poetry from other cultures'. Mary collected these essays in and then redistributed the papers randomly. She then asked the students to identify the significant components of the essay title, which she then set against the qualities that the examiners would be looking for (in this case: structure, language, interest, culture and use of references). She explained that to achieve good grades the students would need to show evidence of all these elements. Next she asked the students to mark in the margin of the piece of work they had before them where they felt the person showed evidence of these elements; finally, they were asked to note anything they felt the person had missed.

The students completed the task in almost complete silence apart from the odd comment, such as 'I haven't done that' or 'I needed to do that'. This illustrates the intimate relationship between peer- and self-assessment. The students were engaged in looking at their peers' work, yet this triggered reflection about the strengths and weaknesses of their own work. The teacher then asked for verbal feedback from the class as a whole. Because of the way in which the peer marking was organized, the students' comments were very focused and relevant (for example, 'They haven't said enough about language' or 'It doesn't cross-refer enough to the cultural context').

Derek at Century Island School wanted to encourage his year 11 students to clarify and organize their ideas on plant nutrition. He began the lesson by getting the students, in groups of four, to do poster-size concept maps for the topic. Groups were then split into two pairs; one pair stayed with their poster, while the other went round the different posters asking the pairs who remained with their poster why they had included some of the terms and why they had linked certain terms together. The pairs in each foursome then swapped places and went round the other seven posters exploring other groups' ideas. This was followed by a 'feedback' session chaired by Derek, where students reported on the terminology selected, paying particular attention to links they thought were good or confusing. When students reported good or confusing links, Derek probed their reasoning.

The students were then given the following question to discuss: 'If a villain got hold of a chemical that could destroy chlorophyll, what effect would this have on plants if released?' Each group of four were asked to write down between three and five criteria that they felt were needed for a good written answer to this question. These criteria were discussed by the whole class and a final list of criteria was drawn up:

- Say what chlorophyll does.
- Explain photosynthesis as a process.
- Put in the equation for photosynthesis.
- Describe effect on plants of no chlorophyll.
- Add any secondary effects from photosynthesis stopping.

The students then wrote up their answers for homework, which Derek then marked by writing comments on their work. He did not allocate grades to the work because he wanted the students to focus and take action on his comments. Students read the comments and each other's work in pairs to check that they understood what the teacher was asking them to do to improve. They were then given time in the lesson to redraft and improve their answer.

Philip, also at Century Island School, was teaching human nutrition, circulation and excretion (a GCSE topic) to a year 10 class. He knew that his class already had a reasonable understanding of nutrition and circulation because of the work that they had done in year 9 and before. Excretion was less familiar to them, so he decided to use the teaching of this topic as a way of linking together all three areas to help his class transfer knowledge from one area to another. He reviewed nutrition and circulation quickly (mainly through a circus of quick practicals, demonstrations and videos). After four one hour lessons and two homeworks (principally questions that checked that the students were getting detailed notes on each part of the work), the students were asked to revise the work done so far for the next lesson. They were told that it was not for a test but for something that required better understanding than a test.

Next lesson, the class were split into groups of five. Each group was given a set of five cards, each of which had one of five words at the top (Absorption, Blood, Circulation, Digestion, Enzymes). The cards were randomly distributed within each group and the students were told that they would have 5 minutes to produce a short oral presentation on that aspect of the topic, which they would then give to the other four members of their group. To help them focus their presentations, underneath each heading were three or four pointers as to what to include. For example, the 'Blood' card bore the following questions:

- What are the main components of blood?
- Briefly what job does the plasma do?
- Briefly what job do the red blood cells do?
- How do white blood cells defend the body against pathogens?

After the preparation time, the teacher stopped the class and told them how they were going to judge each other's presentations in their group. They secretly had to 'traffic light' each presentation and give details to justify their decision as follows:

- *Green*: better than I could have done it/I learnt something from this.
- *Amber*: about the same as I could have done it/no major omissions or mistakes.
- *Red*: not as good as I could have done it/some serious omissions or mistakes.

The members of each group gave their presentation to the group in alphabetical order. No feedback was given within the group until all five presentations had been done. Thus each member of the group judged four presentations and was given feedback from their four peers on their presentation. The suggestions on the cards became rough criteria to support the discussion (and sometimes disagreement about the traffic light given). Through the dialogue, students were able to adopt more sophisticated criteria for their judgements. For example, one of the prompts on the Enzyme card reminded students of the need to 'say what enzymes are'. One student had responded by stating that they were 'biological catalysts'. However, the others in the group decided that he should in addition have said that enzymes were also proteins because that helped later when explaining why enzymes do not function at high temperatures.

Philip then facilitated a 5 minute whole-class discussion in which some students were selected to explain why their presentation had not been awarded 'green' and what they needed to do to improve. Students who accepted that they were 'red' or 'amber' for their presentations were then asked to write out an improved version of their presentation in their books. Those students who were 'green' were asked to select the card that they felt least confident about from the remaining four and do a written presentation of that work. The teacher walked around the classroom as the written work was being completed, stopping at each table and checking with some individuals that they were clear what they needed to include. Those who finished before the end of the lesson were asked to read one another's work to check that they had included all the points.

All these lessons were formative because they created opportunities for students to reveal their own understanding of the criteria for success to their peers and then to improve it. But it is important to note that these opportunities did not arise naturally – they were the result of careful planning and structuring of the lesson by the teachers (see Sadler 1998, p. 83). Piers used the levels of the national curriculum as a basic structure, while Mary used a template of the five properties that she knew that examiners would be looking for in good answers. Derek used the idea of a 'carousel' in which students moved around to look at each other's work and Philip used the idea of traffic lights to structure the students' feedback to each other. In the KMOFAP classrooms, good formative activity was rarely the result of 'on the spur of the moment' ideas, but rather the result of careful planning. It is also worth noting that the group work sessions were successful because the tasks given to the groups had a sharp focus, with clear requirements of the students.

Another feature shared by all four lessons is that while the criteria with which the students worked were not particularly precise, the students were able to make enough sense of the criteria to make specific comments to each other, which helped them learn. In this regard, the students' ability to help each other improve was far more important than the accuracy of their grading of each other's work. In giving feedback to each other, the students began to use the language that they had heard the teacher using when commenting on their own work. This provided them with a 'language of description', which helps students to organize their thinking and provides a tool for analysis. It is also worth noting that this is not confined to older or higher-attaining students, as the following comments on each other's work from a year 8 mixed-ability class demonstrate:

What words does she use to inform you of his isolation?
Very well done. Some of your facts weren't quite write [*sic*] + you
needed to give more examples and quotations. You should have more
topic sentences (the introductory sentence to a new paragraph that
signals a change in topic).

Although in one of these examples students were given a level for their
work, this was not a final level but a trigger for improvement. The students
could accept the idea that their current work was a work in progress and that
they could improve it. Another key feature of all these classrooms is that all the
teachers made lesson time available for the students to work on improvement
(rather than consigning this to a homework activity), which not only showed
how the teacher valued such work, but also allowed students to discuss any
continuing uncertainties with their peers or the teacher.

If effective summative assessment requires that teachers apply a common
standard when assessing students, and form what is often called a 'community
of practice', effective formative assessment requires that students are appren-
ticed into the same community, and the experience of the KMOFAP teachers
suggests that this is achievable in schools. As Ross *et al.* (1993) note, 'students
are capable of rich and sophisticated responses to and understandings of their
own work and seem well able to develop these responses and understandings
in collaboration with their conversation partner' (p. 160).

In addition, engaging in peer- and self-assessment entails much more
than just checking for errors or weaknesses. It involves making explicit what
is normally implicit, thus increasing students' involvement in their own learning. As one student wrote:

> After a student marking my investigation, I can now acknowledge my
> mistakes easier. I hope that it is not just me who learnt from the
> investigation but the student who marked it did also. Next time I will
> have to make my explanations clearer, as they said 'It is hard to
> understand' . . . I will now explain my equation again so it is clear.

So, as well as creating a classroom situation in which the students come to
share with the teacher a feeling of what counts as success (in Guy Claxton's
terms, a 'nose' for quality – Claxton 1995), the KMOFAP teachers and their
students began to move beyond just being able to say *whether* something
was good to being able to say *why*. In other words, they began to develop an
anatomy of quality.

Of course, if students knew where they were in their learning, knew where
they were going and knew what to do about it, then there would be no need
for the teacher to intervene; indeed, one of the benefits of the project reported
by the teachers was that their students became much more autonomous

learners. However, even when the students did not know what to do next, they became much clearer about identifying their own learning needs so that the teacher's help could be understood and put to good use.

Ceri (see next chapter) told us that before she started emphasizing formative assessment, her students would frequently come up to her and say things like 'I can't do quadratics'. When Ceri asked them what it was about quadratics they couldn't do, they would say things like 'I can't do any of it'. Now, she finds her students are much clearer about what they know, and what they don't know and they say things like 'I can't do quadratics when there's a minus in front of the x squared'.

As a consequence of this greater involvement, the students also became much more aware of when they were learning and when they were not. This ability to monitor one's own learning may be one of the most important benefits of formative assessment. After all, while the techniques used by the teachers did improve the students' scores on national curriculum tests and GCSE examinations, very little of what is learned in order to do well on these tests and examinations will be needed later on in life. What is much more important for the long term is that students have acquired the ability to 'learn how to learn' and it is clear that, for most of the students, this was the case (see the comments by Roger Higton in the following chapter)

One class, who were subsequently taught by a teacher not emphasizing assessment for learning, surprised that teacher by complaining: 'Look, we've told you we don't understand this. Why are you going on to the next topic?' While students who are in tune with their learning can create difficulties for teachers, we believe that these are problems we should want to have.

The various aspects of formative assessment also reinforced each other. When teachers successfully developed effective feedback strategies with their students, self- and peer-assessment were further enhanced. Through comment-only marking, the teachers were able to help the students develop attitudes that prioritized how to improve a piece of work rather than in ranking oneself against the performance of others in the class. As we shall see in Chapter 6, different teachers prioritized different things, but a key integrating feature of all of the changes is their focus on identifying and addressing learning needs. This also had consequences for other classrooms in the schools, as students began to challenge teachers who gave them feedback that did not indicate how to improve. As one student said to the teacher, when given a mark of 4 out of 10 for a piece of work: 'How is that going to help me get better?'

Differences between subjects

Comparisons between our experiences of work with teachers of English, science and mathematics have strengthened our view that the subject disciplines create strong differences between both the identities of teachers and the conduct of learning in their classes. Teachers of mathematics and science tend to regard their subjects as being defined by a body of subject matter that gives the subject unique and objectively defined aims. It is possible to 'deliver' the subject matter without necessarily ensuring that students learn with understanding, and even where priority is given to providing help with understanding, it is help that is designed to ensure that every student achieves the 'correct' conceptual goal.

In the teaching of writing, there is very little to 'deliver', except in the case of those rare teachers who focus only on the mechanics in grammar, spelling and punctuation. Rather than a single goal for the whole class, there is a range of goals that might be appropriate for a particular student at a particular time (and, of course, the range of goals will be different for different students at different times). If we view the process of intervening in students' learning as one of 'regulating learning' (i.e. keeping learning on track), then the mathematics and science teachers generally appeared to try to bring all the students in a class to a common goal, while for the English teachers there was a 'horizon' of different goals. Having said this, it is important to note that the English teachers did not operate a policy of 'anything goes'. When a student was pursuing a track that the teacher believed would be unproductive, they did intervene to bring the student back 'on track', but the range of acceptable trajectories of learning seemed to be much greater for English teachers than for the teachers of mathematics and science. It is also important to note that the mathematics and science teachers regulated students' learning in a similar way to the English teachers when their classes were undertaking open-ended activities like investigations or studies of the social and ethical consequences of scientific discoveries.

This suggests that the differences in practice in different subjects are not inherent in the subject, but rather are consequences of the way that the subject is interpreted in the school curriculum. When the goal is very specific, the teacher's regulation of the students' work will be tight; when the goal is less well defined, the regulation will be looser. It is also important to note that this regulation takes place on two levels (as pointed out by Perrenoud 1998). The 'macro' level is that of the task or activity. Where the goal is specific, the teacher will choose a task or activity that will lead students more or less directly to the required skill or competence, but where there is a horizon of possibilities, the task or activity will allow (and perhaps even encourage) different students to head off in different directions. However, the teacher will also regulate learning at the 'micro' level of the individual student, by observing the student's progress and intervening when the student appears not to be 'on track' – and, of course, the more specific the goal, then the tighter the regulation.

The question remains, however, as to whether the differences that emerge in the practices and writing of teachers (see Chapter 6) are merely superficial, and simply arise out of the examples they choose to discuss, or whether assessment for learning is substantially different in different subjects. Some of the perceived differences may be attributable to the fact that teachers of English, at least in secondary schools, are themselves writers and students have more direct interaction with the 'subject', through their own reading and writing, than they do with science and mathematics, for example.

One way of trying to understand the issue is to look at the broad generalizations we might make of different subject areas and the aims and debates that exist within them. At the risk of oversimplification, it is helpful to examine four groups of subjects: the arts, sciences, humanities and languages. Some subjects (e.g. English, technology) could, of course easily be placed within more than one of these groups.

If we begin by considering the arts, it could be said that, among other things, they try to encourage creativity and expression in students. Indicators of success are usually judged by the outcome of the finished product. For some time, however, the process by which this final product is arrived at has been considered important in giving students an experience of what it means to be a practitioner in that subject and also a mechanism by which improvement may be achieved.

If we take English as an example, the significance of process will become clearer. One element of the subject that has been emphasized is the notion of students as writers. This has led to several initiatives, most significantly perhaps the National Writing Project (1989, 1990a,b). To become 'real writers', students were encouraged to engage in the practices of real writers as opposed to simply performing school-based activities. To this end, the project encouraged several practices, including the discussion of ideas and the analysis of generic features of writing, the drafting of work, the use of self- and peer-assessment, a consideration of the audience for whom the work was designed and attempts to broaden that audience beyond the walls of the school.

What emerged, broadly, was a philosophy that placed experimentation and reflection at the heart of practice. Similar observations might be made of art, music, drama and media studies. In drama, the practice of peer feedback on role-playing activities and group performance has been long established and the summative assessments used have reflected this trend. In drama and media studies, students are required to keep a log of the process by which they achieve the final product. Art examinations require previous drafts and designs to be included, as well as a discussion of the process by which designs were made and materials chosen. Coursework in English was introduced largely to enable students to engage in more 'authentic' written tasks (that is, tasks which represent real desired outcomes, rather than proxies).

The debates in these subjects revolve around how the technical and craft aspects involved in the process of creation should be introduced and the extent to which analysis of these technical elements aids performance. In other words, do you have to have the basics first and, if so, what constitutes the basics, or should these so-called 'basics' be introduced within the context of authentic tasks? The same debate appears in the teaching of technology. At one end of the spectrum, there is the view that students must practise the use of different tools, so that they become experts in sawing, planing, sanding and jointing before they actually make anything. At the other is the view that students should learn to use tools in the context of making something of value to the student (a sort of 'just in time' skill development).

Moreover, the subjects in this group also differ in the extent to which they introduce what might loosely be described as the consumption as opposed to the production of works of art. In other words, the extent to which students are asked to study existing music, painting, sculpture, books and so on. In English and media studies, the reading of literature and media texts has usually been given equal weighting with the creation of such texts, although by GCSE, in English at least, they are deemed to be two different subjects and by A-level the notion of students as producers has all but disappeared. In art, drama and music, the emphasis until GCSE is much more strongly biased towards the practical, although the introduction of the national curriculum required students to be introduced to the work of artists and musicians. The study of plays tends to be found in English lessons.

Again, however, emphasis varies on whether teachers are aiming predominantly to encourage the personal response of their students to these works, whether they are honing their critical and analytic faculties or whether works of art are being studied for their canonical value. To an extent these are age-related issues, although the advent of the literacy hour in primary schools has encouraged a much more analytic approach to the study of texts than was previously the case (DfEE 1998, 2001).

Yet whatever the approach taken, until recently the emphasis tended to discourage the idea of a wrong answer. While it has always been perfectly possible to make factual errors in, for example, the description of the plot of a novel, most teachers would still support the notion that as long as an opinion could be supported by evidence and argument, it has some validity (Marshall 2000). The same point could be made in the teaching of history. It may be generally accepted to say that the Second World War started in 1939, but coherent and interesting arguments could be made that the war started in 1937 or 1942, or even 1919.

If we look at these two core aims of arts subjects – the consumption and production of artefacts – we can see that much of the work in which students engage will be of an open-ended nature. No one piece of work will look exactly like another – the imagination cannot be mass-produced or smack of the formulaic. The route by which any child arrives at the finished product will vary and, to an extent, what is important is the reflection or moment of inspiration that has taken place along that route.

On the one hand, this appears to be fertile territory for assessment for learning. Peer- and self-assessment, drafting and reflection are already apparently part and parcel of the picture. On the other hand, teaching the arts seems impossibly 'floaty', the concept of identifiable progression hopelessly nebulous. Interestingly at the heart of the dilemma lies a question of assessment. What makes a good piece of writing? Does the justification for an unorthodox interpretation of a poem work? Is this a poor design and why? Could that student have entered into the role more effectively and if so how? In other words, part of the nature of the subject is to assess quality and learn how to apply those judgements to one's own work. Much of the role of the teacher is to apprentice students into this process. Let us return to the role assessment for learning might play.

To characterize the sciences as the opposite of the arts would be a mistake. Yet the ease by which arts teachers can set open-ended tasks, encourage debate and dissent and see the relevance of this process to their overall aim appears, on the surface, less available in the sciences.

In mathematics, students have to learn to use valid procedures and to understand the concepts that underpin these. Difficulties can arise when they learn strategies that only apply in limited contexts but do not realize that these are inadequate elsewhere. Questioning must then be designed to bring out these strategies for discussion and to explore problems in the understanding of the concepts so that the need to change can be grasped. In such learning, there is usually a well-defined correct outcome. In more open exercises, as in investigations of the application of mathematical thinking to everyday problems, there may be a variety of good solutions; then an understanding of the criteria of quality is harder to achieve and may require an iteration in discussion between examples and the abstract criteria which they exemplify.

In science, the situation is very similar. There are many features of the natural world for which science provides a correct model or explanation. However, outside school, many students acquire different ideas. Examples include the belief that although animals are living, trees and flowers are not because they don't move, or the belief that astronauts seem almost weightless on the moon because there is no air there. Many of these alternative conceptions can be anticipated for they have been well documented. What has also been documented is that mere presentation of the correct view does not change students' beliefs. The task in such cases is to open up discussion of such ideas and then provide feedback that challenges them by introducing new pieces of evidence and arguments that support the scientific model. There are other aspects for which an acceptable outcome is less well-defined. As in mathematics, open-ended investigations call for different approaches to formative assessment. Even more open are issues about social or ethical implications of scientific achievements, for there is no single 'right' answer, and so the work has to be open in a more fundamental way. Then the priority in giving feedback is to challenge students to tease out their assumptions and to help them to be critical about the quality of their own arguments, those of their peers and those that are used elsewhere (in the reporting of science in the media, for example).

The humanities share some features with both the sciences and the arts. The School History Project encouraged students to become historians. Placing less emphasis on the acquisition of historical facts, this initiative asked them to consider the nature of evidence and how that evidence might be pieced together to build a picture of an historical event. Again examination syllabuses followed suit and, instead of relying on multiple-choice and formal essays, students had to examine original sources and comment on their contribution to our understanding. In some respects, the key to this type of teaching lay in encouraging students to ask good questions of the evidence they were being asked to study. Moreover, it enabled teachers to evaluate the extent to which students were grappling with the concepts, be they historical, geographical or philosophical, they were being asked to engage with.

Again we can see how such practice lends itself to the type of activity encouraged by formative assessment. Empathy questions also became staple fare and while some queried whether any student in the twentieth or the twenty-first century could genuinely empathize with a Roman soldier on Hadrian's Wall in the first century, nevertheless the notion of imaginative responses to historical issues gained a foothold. A similar story could be told of religious education and, to an extent, of geography, as in initiatives such as Geography for the Young School Leaver.

Hand in hand with these developments went the continued debate, similar to those that raged around the canon in English, about the extent to which factual information about historical events or geographical facts needed to be taught before any informed argument could be made by a student. Moreover, again as with English, whose history and what geography or religions should be taught has also been fiercely contested.

Language teaching has been similarly torn between an acquisition of the basics through extensive teaching of grammar on the one hand and immersion in the target language and an emphasis on relevance on the other. In our work with the six KMOFAP schools and with others, we have found that modern foreign languages present the greatest challenges in embedding formative assessment into classroom practice. Part of the difficulty is that in classrooms in the UK, there is an orthodoxy that the vast majority of communication between the teachers and the students should take place in the target language. How this orthodoxy has arisen is not clear, but it appears to be based on a mistaken application of the idea of 'immersion' in the target language. There is no doubt that immersion in a language is a very successful method of learning a language. However, it is extremely inefficient in that the total number of hours needed is extremely large. Furthermore, immersing students in a language is impossible in a school context where they are using the language for as little as three hours each week. In some schools, the rigid adherence to immersion means that all the comments written by the teacher in the students' exercise books are in the target language. Of course, the students' competence with the target language is generally not sufficient for them to understand comments in the target language, so that the teacher provides students with a glossary of the comments that she will use for the whole year, which they can keep in their exercise books. This hardly makes for comments attuned to the specifics of a student's work.

If, however, the rigid adherence to the monopoly of the target language is abandoned, then even modern foreign languages create many opportunities for good formative assessment. For example, instead of asking students whether a particular verb is regular (which is a question requiring only factual recall), a teacher could ask what it means for a verb to be irregular – after all, if students do not know the answer to the second question, there is not much point in knowing the answer to the first. When given in English, feedback can be attuned to the details of the student's work, and can make suggestions for what needs to be done.

Modern foreign language teaching also creates many opportunities for sharing criteria with learners and for peer- and self-assessment. In one school, a teacher wanted to improve the students' accent when speaking French. She gave groups of four or five students an extract of French text which was to be read out in the best accent possible. Each group was to get each member of the group in turn to read the piece to the group, and they were then asked to choose the student with the best accent to represent the group in a whole-class plenary. Each group's representative then read the piece and the teacher facilitated a whole class discussion on which of the representatives had the best accent and why. While it was, of course, impossible to make absolutely explicit the features of a good accent, students were helped to improve their accents considerably.

The teaching of modern foreign languages also creates opportunities for self-assessment. In a Spanish classroom, a teacher had collected in letters that the students had written to pen-friends and had underlined each error. She then gave students a grid which listed such common errors as adjective–noun agreement, incorrect definite article and tense and each student had to classify their errors using tally marks. They did this on three occasions. After the third piece of work had been marked in this way, each student had to decide the type of errors they were making most often, set themselves targets for improvement and then identify a 'buddy' in the classroom who had few of these types of error to help them improve.

Like the examples of peer-assessment discussed earlier, these last two examples used carefully thought-out structures to foster effective peer-assessment and to encourage students to reflect on their performance.

If we return to the wider question with which we started this section, we can see that formative assessment is relevant to all school subjects and, although different techniques may be more or less useful in different subjects, all the broad strategies are applicable to all subjects. Provided they are open to new ideas, teachers can learn a great deal by observing good practice in other subjects. For example, the question 'Why is magnesium a metal?' can be seen as a very specific scientific question, but the form of the question is unusual. Rather than asking students to supply the factual recall, the question gives the students the fact and asks them to explain it. This basic form – 'Why is X an example of Y' – can be used as a template for other questions:

- Why is photosynthesis an example of an endothermic reaction?
- Why is a square an example of a rectangle?
- Why is *A Perfect Spy* by John Le Carré an example of a love story?

About half-way through the project, one of the teachers said to us, 'We know why you started with maths and science. We're the remedial group aren't we?' By looking at good formative practice in other subjects (especially physical education and art), they had realized that formative assessment was often well established in other subjects. As James, a teacher at Two Bishops School, observed:

> [other teachers] do more of it than us as part of their normal teaching. Art and drama teachers do it all the time, so do technology teachers (something to do with open-ended activities, long project times and perhaps a less cramped curriculum?).

But ideas developed in mathematics and science classrooms were also taken up in other subjects. James had given a talk to the staff at his school about his experiences, and afterwards a colleague who taught English said to him:

> Yesterday afternoon was fantastic. I tried it today with my year 8s and it works. No hands up and giving them time to think. I had fantastic responses from kids who have barely spoken in class all year. They all wanted to say something and the quality of answers was brilliant. This is the first time for ages that I've learnt something new that's going to make a real difference to my teaching.

Attitudes and beliefs

The work of Carol Dweck (1986) and others has shown that students differ in the ways they attribute their successes and failures to different causes. If students are asked 'When you do well, why is this?' and 'When you do badly, why is this?', then their responses indicate two important underlying distinctions. The first distinction is whether they attribute successes and failures to internal or external factors. For example, 'I got a high mark because I put a lot of work into the task' would be an internal attribution, while 'I got a high mark because the teacher likes me' would be an external attribution. The second distinction is related to the stability of the cause. 'I got a good mark because I'm clever' would be a stable attribution, because the way that most students think of 'cleverness' means that if the reason that you succeeded on something was because you are clever, then you are almost guaranteed a good mark next time, because you'll still be clever. In contrast, 'I did well because I worked hard on this task' is an unstable attribution, because one is not guaranteed success on the next task unless one also works hard on that task. Dweck and others have found that boys tend to attribute their successes to internal stable causes (like ability) and their failure to external unstable causes (like bad luck), whereas girls tend to attribute their successes to internal unstable causes (like effort) and their failures to internal stable causes (like lack of ability).

What is crucial to effective learning is that students attribute both success and failure to internal, unstable causes – in other words, it's down to you and you can do something about it. We should do this even if it were not true, since the consequences are so beneficial, but there is ample evidence to show that it is true. For example, the 2001 'Autumn package' published by the Department for Education and Skills shows that, while those who did well on the key stage 2 tests in 1996 tended also to do well when they took their GCSEs 5 years later, there is a huge degree of uncertainty. Of the students who averaged level 3 or below in their key stage 2 tests, most averaged grade E in their GCSEs 5 years later, but some failed to get any GCSEs and 3 per cent achieved eight grade Bs. For a student who achieves level 4 in each of the tested subjects at key stage 2, all we can say with any certainty is that they will average somewhere between G and A* in their GCSEs. Having said this, it is important that we do not refer to the graphs of such outcomes as 'chances' graphs, since this reinforces the message that success and failure are due to chance, so that the most important ingredient of success is to be lucky on the days of the examinations. Rather, these graphs represent a range of possibilities, and where the student ends up is in no sense pre-determined by current achievement.

Whether students believe this, however, depends in part on their belief in the nature of 'ability'. Some students believe that ability is a fixed entity and that different students have different amounts of this ability. For such students, every task they are set in class is a potential threat to their self-esteem and their goal becomes to preserve this self-esteem. One way to do this is by getting a good mark by whatever means available (including perhaps copying answers from others), and students who are motivated in this way are sometimes referred to as having a 'performance orientation' to their work – the goal in every lesson is not to learn, but to perform well to maintain self-esteem. If, however, a student believes that they are unlikely to be able to succeed on a task, they tend to disengage from the task to protect their self-esteem. In effect, such students would rather be thought of as lazy than stupid. If they do engage in a task and do badly, they will typically attempt to preserve their self-esteem by attributing this failure to external unstable causes, such as bias in the marking, or bad luck.

For students who see ability as dynamic or incremental, a challenging task provides an opportunity to increase one's ability; therefore, whether the belief of the likelihood of ultimate success is strong or not, they will engage with the task to improve their ability. What is interesting is that the same individual may see their ability in, say, mathematics as fixed, while seeing their ability in athletics as incremental in that training improves ability.

This is why the kind of feedback that students receive is so important. As we saw in Chapter 4, much of the feedback received by students is ego-involving and allows them to compare their performance with others. Some do well and others do not, and since it is generally the same students who do well time after time, such feedback systems rapidly establish 'winners' who are confirmed in their success and 'losers' who are confirmed in their failure, which, in turn, reinforces the idea that ability is fixed rather than incremental.

Those who repeatedly receive low marks or grades therefore come to believe that they cannot succeed and tend to disengage from learning. However, there are also dangers for the high-attainers in the competitive classroom. The emphasis on ability as fixed rather than incremental leads to a performance orientation in which they become focused on maintaining their position at the top of the class, and so the high grades and marks become ends in themselves rather than simply indicators that they have learned something well.

By avoiding giving feedback that allowed students to compare their performance with that of their peers, the KMOFAP teachers focused attention on improvement. As well as fostering a notion of ability as incremental rather than fixed, this supported an orientation towards deep learning rather than just getting high marks. In such classrooms, excellence is measured not by what levels are achieved, but by what progress is made. Everyone can succeed, because everyone can improve.

At school level, it is also important that such messages are consistent. Schools that emphasize excellence in achievement run the risk of sending the message that the only students who are valued are those that achieve the highest standards. Students whose performance falls below the highest levels come to believe that they cannot succeed and so disengage. Schools that value excellence in progress are sending the message that everyone can improve, and by feeding back to students about things that are within the students' control, emphasize that further improvement is possible.

For many of the teachers, dispensing with marks and grades was not easy. The students who were used to getting high grades were left uncertain about whether their work was good enough, and they wanted the positive feedback that re-affirmed their self-image as successful students. Perhaps more surprisingly, some of those students who generally got lower marks also found the move away from marks and grades disorienting, presumably because, by attributing these low marks to unstable external factors like bad luck, they hoped that eventually their luck would turn and they would get a good grade or mark. It is important to realize how disorienting this can be for students and that they need to understand the reasons for any changes in practice.

Peer-assessment has a role to play here, too. Many of the teachers found that students were much tougher on each other than they, the teachers, would dare to be. Feedback from peers is less emotionally 'loaded' than feedback from those in authority and is more easily accepted as well. Several teachers also found that students cared more about communicating with their peers than they did with the teacher, so that their work became neater when they knew that it would be read by their peers.

Finally, observations of peers explaining things to each other revealed important insights about why this is such a powerful process. Students often communicated complex ideas in a language that was different from what the teacher would have used, but appeared to be more easily assimilated by other students. When explaining things to each other, students often interrupted the peer's explanation asking them to repeat something, which the teachers told us never happened when it was the teacher doing the explaining. And students also told us that after the second explanation of something from a teacher, they pretended they understood when they did not. Some did this because they were aware of how busy the teacher was and did not feel they had the right to monopolize the teacher's time, while others did so because they did not want to appear stupid in front of the teacher. Whatever the reason, the result was that because of the involvement of ego in the learning situation, the learning was less effective. However, when students received help from each other, they asked for repeated explanations until they had understood.

Peer-assessment and peer-tutoring is not a strategy for coping with inadequate student–teacher ratios – indeed, it can often secure better learning than would be achieved with one teacher for each student.

Research into learning

If what we were claiming here were entirely new or radical, we could have little faith that our findings would be generalizable beyond the schools involved in the KMOFAP project. However, it is clear that our findings are entirely consistent with a broad range of research in education and psychology. Any study of how learning is understood in the light of recent research will emphasize the importance of the issues raised in this chapter (see, for example, Wood 1998; National Research Council 1999). Thus this research emphasizes the importance of such general principles as:

- the need to start from a learner's existing understanding;
- the need to involve the learner actively in the learning process;
- the importance of meta-cognition, which calls both for a judgement of one's present understanding and for a clear view of the purpose of the learning and of the criteria for judging achievement of that purpose;
- the importance of the social element of learning which is made effective through interaction in discussion.

To take only the last example, a vast amount of research building on the work of the Russian psychologist Lev Vygotsky has shown the importance of language in all cognitive development. It is by talking about their thinking as it emerges that thinking is reinforced and developed:

> external and social activities are gradually internalised by the child as he comes to regulate his own intellectual activity. Such encounters are the source of experiences which eventually create the 'inner dialogues' that form the process of mental self-regulation. Viewed in this way, learning is taking place on at least two levels: the child is learning about the task, developing 'local expertise'; and he is also learning how to structure his own learning and reasoning.
>
> (Wood 1998, p. 98)

Additionally, and to some surprisingly, there are also many studies which present sound research evidence that the kinds of feedback typical in schools are frequently counterproductive. Examples include:

- Students told that feedback 'will help you to learn' more than those told that 'how you do tells us how smart you are and what grades you'll get'; the difference is greatest for low attainers (Newman and Schwager 1995).
- Those given feedback as marks are likely to see it as a way to compare themselves with others (ego-involvement); those given only comments see it as helping them to improve (task-involvement): the latter group out-perform the former (Butler 1987, 1988; Butler and Neuman 1995).
- In a competitive system, low attainers attribute their performance to lack of 'ability', high attainers to their effort; in a task-oriented

system, all attribute it to effort and learning is improved, particularly among low attainers (Craven *et al.* 1991).

- A comprehensive review of research studies of feedback showed that feedback improved performance in only 60 per cent of them. In the cases where it was not helpful, the feedback turned out to be merely a judgement or grading with no indication of how to improve (Kluger and DeNisi 1996).

It is also clear that the practices adopted by the KMOFAP teachers would be recognizable as what was being advocated as 'good practice' by Her Majesty's Inspectors of Schools in the 1970s and 1980s. In this sense, hardly any of the individual techniques and strategies that the KMOFAP teachers are using are new.

What is new is that formative assessment provides ways for teachers to create classrooms that are more consistent with the research on learning. A focus on formative assessment does not just add on a few techniques here and there – it organizes the whole teaching and learning venture around learning, and supports teachers in organizing the learning experiences of their students more productively. This theme is taken up in Chapter 8. In the next chapter, we look in more detail at the way that involvement in the KMOFAP project changed teachers, students and the relationship between them.

6 Changing yourself

Implementing assessment for learning requires personal change. It means changing the way a teacher thinks about their teaching and their view of their role as a teacher. Since the way a teacher teaches is inextricably linked with their own personality and identity, ultimately it means changing yourself. Teachers told us that these changes happened slowly – almost imperceptibly – as they became aware of the implications of placing formative assessment at the heart of their teaching, but when they looked back the cumulative effect was substantial.

As one of the KMOFAP teachers said, assessment for learning is 'a way of thinking, almost a philosophy'. For most teachers, this way of thinking contrasts strongly with the focus on teaching 'performance' that has been the largely unintended result of government initiatives in recent years. Teachers who are emphasizing formative assessment change their underlying beliefs about what counts as 'good teaching'. Their focus is less on teaching and more on the learning in their classroom. Specifically, plans are evaluated in terms of how far those actions will enhance the students' learning and how explicitly they will inform the teacher and the students about what is being learnt. This change in the way that the KMOFAP teachers thought about their teaching changed the role of everyone in the classroom: the role that they took as a teacher and their expectations of the role that their students would take.

That every teacher starts at a different point is self-evident, but we also found that teachers followed different trajectories of change – so not only their starting points, but also the routes they travelled were different. For most of the teachers, the stimulus for change was one or more of the classroom techniques that had been highlighted by research into formative assessment. Although some teachers embraced a range of techniques, for others a single idea acted as a 'Trojan horse' in promoting an extensive change in their practice. For example, with one teacher the desire to provide effective feedback led to a more careful evaluation of the kinds of tasks set, which, in turn, led to an awareness of the need to make the criteria for success as clear as possible.

Not every teacher travelled the same distance, and there were certainly differences in the extent to which all their actions were focused on learning. Some teachers needed to build up confidence in the use of formative assessment by taking small steps, and some were apprehensive because of a difficulty of seeing how things could be different. In other cases, teachers were not sure that they had enough subject knowledge to be able to interpret the answers given by students in open whole-class questioning. However, even when teachers used only one or two of the ideas of formative assessment, this did have an impact on their students' achievement.

For teachers who are interested in exploring formative assessment and who are interested in knowing what it involves, we believe that the best source of evidence is from the teachers themselves. In this chapter, therefore, we look in detail at the practices of some of the KMOFAP teachers and how their classrooms changed. We begin by describing the ways in which five teachers changed. For two teachers, Derek and Ceri, we draw on our own observations to show how they followed very different trajectories. This is followed by personal accounts from three teachers, Katrina Harrell, Barbara Eggleton and Roger Higton (their real names!), about their involvement with the project, reflecting on what formative assessment has meant to them. The chapter then looks more generally at the changes in the role of teachers that embrace formative assessment, at the related changes in the role of students and, finally, at the risks and rewards that go with these changes.

Stories of teacher change

Two different trajectories

In this section, we describe the changes in the practice of two teachers, Derek and Ceri. Derek was a science teacher with about 10 years teaching experience when he joined the KMOFAP project. He was very impressed by the evidence put forward in the INSET sessions and very much wanted to be involved. He saw formative assessment as the way to improve the learning of his students. However, many aspects of formative assessment represented considerable challenges for him. He had developed a style of teaching that required him to work very hard in lessons. When he was observed by one of us (C.L.), the pace was frenetic. He asked quick-fire questions that required brief answers; there were no silences in the classroom, no lull in the proceedings to allow for reflection. One activity followed another, with Derek relentlessly making sure that the students were busily occupied. He felt at this time that the only way he could find out about every student's learning needs would be to conduct individual interviews. His action plan settled on comment-only marking and questioning as the main techniques he wanted to develop. Focusing on feedback to individuals in the form of comments meant that he responded to the students on an individual basis, while for questioning he worked on his questions with a colleague. He chose to start off by concentrating on his teaching performance, thinking about what he did, about how he responded to the students rather than thinking about how the students responded to what he offered.

Ceri was very different. Her profile in her lessons was much more low-key than Derek's. She thought hard about her students and tried to respond to them as well as she could. She was a successful and experienced mathematics teacher and her experience had led her to believe that regular and frequent testing was the best way to help her students do well in external examinations. She marked everything that her students did and recorded those marks conscientiously. Through her involvement in the project, she came to see that this was not enough. While her students needed to know what they could do, they also needed to know how to improve. In her action plan, therefore, she concentrated on self-assessment so that her students could know what they could do but also what they needed to know. She began to use strategies so that the students could tell *her* 'what they need to know' and she could then work with them to help them to know more.

> It's much more extending this idea of them telling me what they need to learn. I think it helps that you are not telling them what you think they got wrong and they need to go over; they are telling you what things they can't do.
>
> (Ceri, Two Bishops School)

These two teachers have made huge changes to their classrooms. They have taken up the ideas of formative assessment and have used them to improve the learning in their classes. They have changed many of their practices and have talked about changes in their values and beliefs as professional teachers. However, they are still very different. Ceri focuses on the students and encourages them to assess themselves and thereby provide her with the information she needs to plan future lessons. When she began teaching a module on 'Shape and space' to a year 7 class, she asked the students to write down everything they knew about quadrilaterals and discovered they already knew everything she had planned and quickly replanned the lesson. She set her year 11 group a question that required the cosine rule to solve it, let them work out that a solution was not possible with their existing knowledge and why, and then taught them what they needed – another example of 'just-in-time' teaching. She allows her students to assess their own learning needs and then works with them to meet those needs. However, she still uses summative tests, which she uses to rank students so that they can see where they are against others in the year. This seems to us an important feature of the way that we worked with teachers. Because there was no 'package' of techniques that teachers had to adopt wholesale, they were free to retain aspects of their practice to which they were strongly committed and adopt those practices with which they felt comfortable.

Derek also came to develop his use of self-assessment strategies with students, but for him this came later. He now sees self-assessment as important, but his main focus has been and remains questioning and his use of comment-only marking. The most obvious change in his practice is in the way he values the thoughtful responses of the students he teaches. The latest observations of Derek's teaching show him to be an expert at questioning; the style of his questions and the pace of his lessons invite full thoughtful answers from his students. These answers allow Derek access to his students' understanding and he could be seen to be tailoring his teaching in response to his students' needs. The difference from the rushed lessons we saw at the start of the project, where he hardly allowed time for students to think, could hardly be more marked.

These changes in the practice of these two teachers were attributable to the reflection on their own practice, which was structured by new ideas from research, by interaction with others and by feedback from observations. The teachers were able to use perspectives other than their own to help them to articulate a clear vision of the way that they wished their teaching to develop. The regular observations with feedback from the King's team and their own colleagues contributed enormously to the changes we have seen. The teachers were also asked to think deeply about planning their next steps and to review their thoughts at regular intervals during and between the INSET sessions, activities which promoted reflection. The information given over time, often in response to requests from the teachers themselves, also contributed to the process of reflection. The way that this information was provided by the King's team assumed that the teachers were committted to constant improvement. The teachers saw themselves as part of a quest to improve the learning of their students.

Both Derek and Ceri felt that some of the changes they had to make were 'risky'. Derek, in his personal journal, described how dangerous it felt to leave empty time for the students to think of an answer to his questions. In an interview, Ceri spoke of the need to change the way she controlled lessons, but admits to feelings of uncertainty in doing so. They, in common with other KMOFAP teachers, are now talking about changes in what might be called the locus of control (see below). They talk about having to let go, about letting the students take over control of, or some responsibility for, the progress of the lesson:

> But you do, you have to, you have to allow them the freedom to take the lesson their way for a little while and then pull it back together. And I think there are times when you think, are they getting as much done as you would expect them to be getting through? And I think

> perhaps they don't get as much written down but it's probably, the understanding's probably better by the fact they have shared the ideas and the thinking time but it's not such tight control.
>
> (Ceri, Two Bishops School – March 2000)

Allowing the students to take control of their learning seems to be a big step. Derek was very reluctant to take it. When Ceri decided she had to take it, she spoke strongly about the feelings of insecurity that this engendered in her. Another of the teachers, Tom, felt that he could only fulfil his obligations to the students if he did take this step. All of our teachers said at the start that they wanted the students to take responsibility for their learning but they felt that the students would not or could not do this. Now, as they have come to understand the implications of the ideas of formative assessment, they realize that the students can take this responsibility and can take some control, but they must be taught how to do this: teachers cannot make students do it just by wishing that they would.

During the project, we encouraged teachers to keep journals to help them maintain a focus on formative assessment and also to help them reflect on their practice as it developed. We also asked each of the teachers to write a summary of their involvement in the project; three of these summaries are given below. In reading these accounts, it is important to bear in mind that these were not struggling teachers who suddenly found a 'magic lamp' that transformed their practice. They were skilled and reflective teachers who were prepared to take on practices that would enable them and, more importantly, their students to be even more successful. They saw the potential in formative assessment to allow their students to become good, self-monitoring learners, which is, of course, a skill teachers want their students to acquire.

Katrina Harrell, head of an English department

Katrina joined the project as part of the English extension to the project in Autumn 2000. Although many of the techniques of formative assessment were well established in her classroom, she nevertheless found that there were things that a systematic focus on formative assessment could contribute to her practice.

> The Formative Assessment project was already well underway in the maths and science faculties when I attended an introductory meeting. Here, representatives were reflecting on the benefits of techniques such as asking open questions and using assessment criteria with students. I must admit that I was somewhat sceptical about the project, since these techniques were already part and parcel of our practice in the English faculty.

My scepticism, however, quickly dissipated with the opportunities that the project offered both to analyse and reflect on my own practice and that of other colleagues. Such professional dialogue is invaluable to all teachers and, indeed, the insights gleaned have proved to be illuminating in many ways.

The project has encouraged me to think about what assessment really means; it is too often associated with a summative process whereby the student has little opportunity to rectify or improve their work. I believe that an effective teacher, however, continually assesses the students' learning in order to move their learning forward. The project has raised my awareness of the many ways that I assess students in the classroom and has underlined the importance of sharing the assessment process with them and, indeed, inviting them to participate in it.

Placing the student in the role of teacher in this way has proved to be a powerful learning tool. I have introduced more systematic peer-marking into my teaching since I have been on the KMOFAP project and this has been adopted by the whole faculty. We have incorporated opportunities for peer-marking in our schemes of work and have also devised drafting checklists for students to use before they hand in a piece of written work. We insist that we see evidence of the students' own corrections on the work before we look at it. This has encouraged the students to become more independent learners, a key focus of formative assessment.

We have learnt that in order to implement peer- and self-marking we have to share assessment criteria very explicitly with the students. They need to understand exactly what is required of them in order to improve their work. To this end, we have produced simplified and pupil-friendly examination assessment criteria on laminated cards. The students really enjoy the challenge of such an activity and, by becoming so involved in the assessment process, what they learn tends to stay with them.

Of course, self- and peer-marking is not a substitute for our marking, but a complement to it; there are times when we have to mark students' work and award levels or grades. It has long been obvious to me that students' primary concern when work is returned is their level of attainment rather than how they might improve. I was therefore more than happy to trial comment-only marking with my teaching groups. The students soon got used to this and I'm convinced that their work improved as a consequence. The results were especially noticeable in lower attainers, since grades can often have a de-motivating effect with such students, which can be extremely destructive to their self-esteem. During the project I incorporated this aspect of formative assessment into the faculty's marking and assessment policy so that it is now commonplace both at key stages 3 and 4.

We have also discussed in the faculty the importance of allowing structured thinking time for students. I began by trying to give increased wait time when asking questions but found that the same students answered anyway! Since then, I have adapted the approach and now regularly ask students to confer in pairs for one minute before feeding back to the whole class. This has not only been very successful in encouraging some of the less confident students to contribute, but has also elicited much richer responses from the whole class.

Finally, the project has impressed upon me the need to encourage independence in students; too often they expect to be passively 'spoon-fed' a syllabus, while we succeed not in extending their creativity but in quashing it. By the careful use of questioning, by encouraging students to critically reflect on their own and on others' work and by making them partners in the teaching and learning process, I believe we can make a real difference for the better.

Barbara Eggleton, head of a mathematics department

Barbara was one of the original twenty-four teachers and has been a keen and reflective member of the project from the start. As she was head of the mathematics department, she was in a position to influence directly the practice of other teachers as well as her own. Once she was sure that the ideas worked in her own classroom, she shared them with others in her department and encouraged them to do the same. Recently, she has moved to a new school that has presented new challenges. She remains convinced of the importance of formative assessment to a high standard of education for the students in her charge and is facing the challenges of disseminating these ideas once again.

The main thrust of the KMOFAP project became a simple one for me: opening up the learning process and sharing it with my students. My simplified version of 'opening the black box' became increasingly important and powerful in my teaching and in their learning. Teaching and learning became inextricably interlinked in a way that I had not managed before.

At the start of the project, my action plan contained three strands: developing group work for exploring assessment criteria, reflecting on work covered and developing good questions. However, in practice, all three became one as I developed my thinking. I have since moved to a different school at the other end of the country and I am forced to reflect on my practice as I meet new students who are unfamiliar with my ways. The school I now teach in is a grammar school and I find that students who have already achieved well in a 'traditional' classroom are not so keen to get involved with their learning on a grand scale! Together with leading a department of teachers who are unused to the ideas of formative assessment, this has forced me to examine what I think is most important and to start from scratch in some ways.

The first time I asked a year 10 top set to work in groups to examine the errors they had made in a test and to help each other to understand fully what was being asked of them, it was unsuccessful. They were not used to the ethos of taking that level of responsibility. That lesson I heard several times, 'Why don't you just tell us?' I had designed the groups carefully, with mixed-ability pairings (two top with two middle, two middle with two bottom) to maximize the potential of this approach. I found myself justifying these tactics over and over again, in a way that I did not have to do with younger groups who were more accepting of the idea of working together to enhance understanding. I had to work hard to get the year 10 group to see assessment as a way of improving learning, not a series of snapshot judgements about achievement and progress. I needed them to see that their actual test scores were not the issue; what we did about improving their understanding was much more important.

However, I persevered and that particular class is now much clearer about what they are trying to achieve. They now ask to go into groups after exams and naturally work with each other to improve their understanding. They give me feedback, both orally and written, about their understanding; they decide, with me, if we are ready to move on or if more time would be beneficial; they correct every piece of work, although not always in groups, more often in pairs. They are more open to challenges and do not expect me to 'spoon-feed' them with techniques, which they can regurgitate in exams. They are becoming better, more deeply thinking, mathematicians as a result. I realized that my way of teaching is unfamiliar to them and they have realized that they have more to do in my classroom than absorb the syllabus – they have to take responsibility for their learning. So what is this 'unfamiliar' approach?

On a practical level, I try to open up the learning process for the students by sharing the learning objectives, discussing mark schemes, encouraging self- and peer-assessment during coursework. A successful student then feels empowered and aware of what he or she is trying to achieve. The students are not totally reliant on me to gradually disclose the course to them.

However, that is only one part of it. The students need to be able to reflect on their understanding and to communicate with me in a way that helps them to improve. The simple idea of a traffic light on each piece of work is a great starting point. Now all my students take time to reflect on their understanding and then decide if they are red, amber or green. In itself, this is a useful process as they are deciding for themselves, not waiting for me to tell them if they understand. However, it becomes more powerful if their feedback is then used to plan future lessons. I record traffic lights for each student in my mark book. It is so much more visual than a mark (a practice I was never comfortable with) and it comes in useful in all sorts of ways. When revising, I can group students according to their own perceived understanding, I can pinpoint topics where there are still some students who are amber. Their ambition is to 'go green' through whatever means possible and I have to facilitate that.

The other element that developed during the project was my questioning. One interesting study showed that our body language as questioners led to the students trying to guess what was in our head when really our questions should be probing to find out what is in theirs. By accepting every oral answer with the same body language and then asking another student to comment on it, the programmed responses of students are challenged. (What is the answer? is that right? why is it right/wrong?) The ethos in the class has to be right – non-judgemental and all striving for understanding – and when it is, this opens up so much discussion and teases out misunderstandings. Most mathematics teachers use mental and oral starters now and all of us are trying to become more skilled in the way that we do this, but we need to be sure that, in doing so, we are moving along the learning of every student. Quick-fire questioning without time for reflection and examining misconceptions may have the opposite effect. Well-planned questions, which are not afraid to challenge students' long-held methods, can be very powerful.

I have met and taken on board ideas that work for me, which enhance what I was already trying to do and from which I see obvious benefits for the students. I have also met ideas which I found hard to manage or which I only attempt occasionally. However, the discussions about learning and assessment have added a richness to what I do as a teacher and given me a better understanding of what it means to be a successful learner.

Roger Higton, science teacher and head of year

Roger was one of the original cohort of teachers on the project. He was an accomplished and reflective teacher at the start of the project, so that the ideas of formative assessment challenged his idea of himself. Was he prepared to take a risk and change his practice when it was working well already? As we see, he was, and he was prepared to go through a difficult patch when both his students and himself seemed to be achieving less than they did. He changed fundamentally the way that he thought about teaching and developed an approach that measurably improved the learning that went on in his classroom.

> Good assessment for learning involves a two-way dialogue between both student and teacher; each not only listening to what the other is saying, but using what is said to inform the learning process. This method not only changed, fundamentally, the way that I taught, but also it changed the way my students took charge of their own learning process. Briefly, formative assessment gave me the confidence and the tools to climb down from the position of a 'presenter of knowledge', to one where I could use my skills as a teacher more creatively. Everyone in the classroom arrived at an understanding of the ecology of teaching and learning, and what is more – it was fun. The use of the word ecology (which is the science of the interaction between organisms and their environment) is an attempt to describe the new dynamics in the classroom. We all had to be aware of everyone else, be prepared not just to listen, but to listen with an empathetic ear, we all had to understand and invest in a common goal, which was to move learning forward.
>
> Assessment for learning has given me a greater insight into the interactions between myself and my students. They, in turn, became more aware of what I was trying to do; they began to help me to help them learn. Rather than me just being involved in 'crowd control' and the dispensing of knowledge, there developed a partnership between myself and my students, based on mutual respect and trust; one where all felt comfortable with being challenged and where we could all make mistakes. We were all responsible for what went on in the classroom, and an understanding of this responsibility played its own part in raising achievement and making the whole process of teaching more satisfying.
>
> Of course, this process did not happen by accident. I teach in a fully comprehensive school, to mixed-ability groups; it took time for my target group to accommodate this new ecology and there were times when I wondered whether the struggle was worth it! During my involvement with the project, I kept a diary where I recorded each lesson, what I was doing and how I was going to bring formative assessment techniques into the lessons. At the end of each session I recorded, in red, my observations and evaluation of the lesson itself. An early entry read 'I feel that the standards of the group are falling.

Effort and neatness reduced – but are they learning more? Where is the reference point?' It was clear that new ways of working together with new boundaries had to be established and to do this successfully took all my skills as a teacher.

Next, new techniques had to be mastered, thus scrawled across the entry for 20th September 1999 was the phrase 'NO MORE GRADES' – here I had written my statement of intent. The first evidence of the positive impact formative assessment would make came on the next entry. Written, rather neatly, in red was 'Marked books, very pleased with outcome. Did not use grades. Lots of merits given, because quality of analysis v. good'. Here was the evidence that kept me going – formative techniques were beginning to work and soon the students felt this success. They recognized that within the classroom there was not only an expectation to learn, but that they would be helped in this process. So, very early on I was getting evidence of the positive effect formative assessment was having on learning in my lessons. The work I marked was better.

Assessment for learning held the key to good teaching, it was child-focused and it had learning and teaching at its centre, but in the early stages it was hard work. One entry read: 'difficult to change the culture to focusing on wrongs rather than what is right'. This entry acknowledged that formative assessment requires students to change their approach to their own learning; they had to become more proactive. The ecology of the learning environment becomes based on mutual support and a spirit of cooperation. This gave an environment where students felt safe to give wrong answers and to express, freely, their lack of understanding. Here the classroom ceased to be a habitat where only the brightest survived and flourished, but one where, with careful grouping and good questioning, every student could feel themselves making progress through the lesson.

Assessment for learning will only work if it enhances teaching and learning. Students will not invest in its practice if it does not bring them a reward. They are taking risks by allowing themselves to be questioned in a more rigorous manner. Another diary entry notes 'students worked well with close questioning', and they did work well because the questioning was there to assess their learning needs. Two months later I wrote, 'they themselves seem to be becoming more confident learners. Attitudes changing faster in some than others, need to tackle "quiet-head-down" low achievers. It has become unacceptable in groups to be loud-low-achievers. Loud-high-achievers the norm'.

What else needs to be said? Their enthusiasm as year 9 students led them to achieve higher than expected results in their key stage 3

.ter, as sixth-form students, they
. the lessons where they understood,
.at learning was about.

T   are by no means untypical of the changes
in the   )FAP. By looking across all forty-eight of the
teach   .? project, we can see that the changes in their
pract   .ıny aspects of the classroom. Specifically, what
chang   .: views about learning, their professional priorities, t.   .ɪeir students and their feelings about control in
their cla

Changes .ɪn   .acher's role

Putting learnɪ.ɪɟ

All the KMOFAP teachers reported that they changed the way that they
thought of their teaching. They now think of their teaching in terms of facilitating students' learning, rather than feeling that they have to 'get through'
the curriculum at all costs. The teachers saw the purpose of their lessons as
primarily to help students learn – if the students did not learn, then they had
to rethink the lesson and try another way.

> Because there is so little curriculum time, it's very easy to think – 'I've
> got to get on, I've got to teach this, this and this and if I don't teach
> this I'm not going to have enough time to teach that'. It's very, very
> easy to teach lots of things very badly, well not very badly but so that
> you are getting through a lot of stuff but there is actually not a lot
> of learning going on. So what I am trying to do is, the point I am
> emphasizing is, I don't really mind how little you do as long as you
> actually teach people stuff, as long as there is demonstrable learning
> going on and you are satisfied that you are improving skills and
> understanding.
>
> (Deputy head, Two Bishops School)

This demanded several changes to the approach that many of our teachers
were taking, most importantly thinking of the content as a series of learning
goals rather than a series of activities to be completed. By setting out clearly in
their own minds what they wanted the students to learn, the teachers would
be in a position to find out what the 'gap' was between the state of the students' current learning and the learning goal and to be able to monitor that
'gap' as it closed. Thinking of the curriculum as a set of goals to be learned is an
important change in thinking about teaching.

As a result, one of the ways in which teachers changed the way they thought of their teaching was to focus much more about meeting learning needs rather than about delivering a set curriculum. The curriculum dictates the topic to be learned and the learning goals, but the needs of their students dictates the pace and style of the lessons. One teacher said that they were prepared to teach only two-thirds of the curriculum designated for a given year if that amount was learned well. Teachers were prepared to spend the time that was needed to make sure that their students fully understood something before moving on to another area of the curriculum. However, in practice, it was rarely necessary for teachers to omit parts of the curriculum, because for every topic that needed more time spent on it to cover it properly, there was another that the students knew about already and could be covered quickly.

This approach highlighted the need for teachers to be aware of the 'big picture' in the area that they are teaching. They needed to be able to use a full range of content knowledge. It didn't work if they saw each lesson or group of lessons in isolation from others. They needed to know where the idea or skill that they wished their students to learn in the immediate future fitted into the larger whole of that subject. That way they were able to supply missing ideas or deal with troublesome misconceptions if students were having trouble getting started with the lesson, or they were able to go quickly to further or deeper learning if the planned material had already been learnt. The teachers that we worked with had great enthusiasm for and knowledge of their subject – we do not think this is unusual. The KMOFAP teachers saw themselves as the people who are expected to think through the learning and who can subdivide the big picture into parts that their students can manage in the time available, while not losing sight of the whole.

Although formative assessment undoubtedly makes considerable demands on a teacher's subject knowledge, this does not mean that formative assessment can only be used by subject 'experts'. When teachers have the confidence to explore ideas with their students, then different conceptions can emerge from the discussions between students. However, knowing the subject well does mean that the teacher is more likely to be able to ask a probing question, as in the following example, already quoted on p. 35 of a teacher who started a new unit by having:

> an in-depth question and answer session – with open-ended, challenging questions – such as, 'If plants need sunlight to make food, how come the biggest plants don't grow in deserts, where it's sunny all the time?' A *far better* lead in to the recall of photosynthesis than, 'What is the equation for photosynthesis?' The former question allows all those students who don't even remember the word photosynthesis to begin formulating ideas and to be part of a discussion

> that gradually separates those who do remember and understand photosynthesis from those who don't.
>
> > (Philip, Century Island School; teacher's emphasis)

This quotation also illustrates Philip's approach to ensuring that all students are included in the learning. The formative teacher will be looking for ways that allow everyone in their classes to know that their voice is valued. Teachers practising formative assessment make sure everyone is invited to speak and that a student's expression of problems is responded to in an appropriate fashion, every time. Such teachers listen to their students and take care to select activities that make it possible for them to listen to everyone and act on what they hear.

> I now use the 'hands down' strategy and this has made a big difference to my classroom discussions. In particular, it has broadened the range of participation and removed (at its best) the curious mixture of envy and relief which characterized the mood of a group while the usual people answered questions. In a word, discussions are now much more inclusive and much more scary!
>
> > (Paul, Cornfields School)

Put simply, the KMOFAP teachers think of their teaching as responding to the actual learning needs of all of the students and making it possible for themselves and their students to find out what these needs might be. In the process of increasing the students' awareness of the state of their own learning, teachers can improve their own awareness and will use their professional expertise to move that learning forward.

Another aspect of the role of teachers focusing on formative assessment is that they do not see themselves as deliverers of facts or as someone who certifies that students have had the opportunity to hear and possibly learn. They have to help all students to learn what is 'delivered' and to achieve this challenging aim they have to seek out ways to help themselves become more adept at their task. They talk to other teachers about good practice, sharing questions that may reveal much about a topic or about misconceptions that students have. They seek out activities and ideas that have the capacity to help students learn. They talk about ways to organize their classroom so that the students are able to assess each other as they come to know about a concept and therefore enable each student to monitor their own progress. They read and reflect on educational research evidence and act on it where appropriate. It is our experience that these teachers, no matter how skilled they are at their job, look for ways to make themselves even better.

A department focusing on improving formative practice will:

- Have an atmosphere in which teachers are expected to watch other teachers in action – the cover system will actively support peer observation.
- Recognize and value current skills and help teachers to identify their current formative practice.
- Have meetings where teachers discuss learning.
- Give teachers time to plan well by encouraging them to mark less, but mark better.

(Derek, Century Island)

The teachers in the KMOFAP project understood that to act in this professional way, they needed not only to *respond* to the way that their students learnt in their classrooms but to begin to *anticipate* the students' needs as well (hence the request for a session on learning mentioned in Chapter 3).

Changes in a teacher's expectations of their students

As the project progressed, many of the teachers moved away from a perception of their students as having a fixed level of ability to see them as being able to improve with appropriate help and support – a shift from a fixed to an incremental view of ability as discussed in Chapter 5. If the required learning did not seem to be happening, the teachers thought about a different approach and gave the students more time to come to an understanding. The teachers did not think that the students were unable to understand because of some inherent deficiency in those students.

However, the teachers did expect students to take some responsibility for their learning. The idea (prevalent in the 1960s and 1970s) that, provided the teacher did a reasonable job, whether students succeeded or failed was out of the teacher's control, has been substantially discredited in recent years, which is a very positive development. On the other hand, it may be that the pendulum has swung too far the other way, since many of the teachers described feeling that accomplishing learning in the classroom was entirely their responsibility – a feeling exacerbated by the pressure they felt to improve their students' performance on national curriculum tests and GCSE examinations.

Despite these swings in beliefs and practices, the evidence from research about learning is that there is no choice. The students are the ones that have to do the learning; the teacher knows that they cannot do the learning for the students:

> It became obvious that one way to make a significant sustainable change was to get the students doing more of the thinking. I then began to search for ways to make the learning process more transparent to the students. Indeed, I now spend my time looking for ways to

get students to take responsibility for their learning at the same time making the learning more collaborative.

(Tom, Riverside School)

One of the teachers, when asked about what she had gained from involvement in the project, replied that she was almost embarrassed to say. When pressed she said, 'I've realized it's not about teaching, it's about learning'. Under pressure to 'do better' it seemed that many of the teachers had assumed more and more of the responsibility for their students' learning. The opportunities for reflection created within the KMOFAP project allowed the teachers to realize that, while teachers had a key role in organizing learning experiences, they could not do the learning for their students. So, for example, in classroom questioning, every student would be expected to have an opinion and be prepared to express it:

> Most lessons opened with a 'big question' which had to be worthy of thought and have a range of possible responses. The students were getting used to the idea and were increasingly prepared to offer responses when they were unsure. I have also started to move away from hands up. The class knows that they will all contribute at some point and most responses are requested by me rather than volunteered. Sometimes I'll open it up to the group and, occasionally, someone is desperate to speak, especially if another student has just ripped their dearly held theory apart.
>
> (James, Two Bishops School)

Replies that demonstrate a misconception are more important than correct ones, as they provide an opportunity to extend learning both for that student and for others in the class who may well share the same misconception. Students who do not get involved in such exchanges are not just harming themselves, they are also failing to help the learning of the others in the class.

Within such a view, it is the student's responsibility to monitor and manage their own learning and to alert the teacher to problems. Teachers do not expect their students to do this without help, but it is a vital building block in formative practice. A teacher engaging with formative assessment sets out to include all students in the learning and also to meet the learning needs of them all. Self-monitoring is an essential element in this. As one teacher put it, 'in a class of thirty it becomes blindingly obvious that the students must monitor themselves' (Tom, Riverside School). For the KMOFAP teachers to do their job in the way that they saw they must, they devised ways for the students themselves to supply the information that they, as their teacher, needed to know (for example, the traffic lights used by Barbara).

The teachers also sought to minimize competition between students, since it can breed complacency in those that are able to meet the learning criteria easily and make those who often find learning difficult feel demoralized. Minimizing competition also supports collaboration between students. Peer tutoring was used as a way to enhance collaboration, but a collaborative atmosphere requires more than that. It calls for a classroom in which everyone is working together to move learning forward. For example, in collaborative questioning sessions, teachers made clear that when students expressed their own ideas and issues, they helped others clarify their thoughts. Competition to be the one that gives the right or 'clever' answer does not have the same learning potential.

The teachers also expected their students to do more thinking in lessons. They planned lessons carefully so that there was a better balance between the thinking that a teacher does during the lesson and the thinking that the students do. Students learn when they are actively engaged in the ideas and when they reflect. That is, the more thinking they do in the lesson, the more they learn. Formative assessment demands that the students think about their learning and also that they express their learning verbally. It is only through students expressing their learning that both they and the teacher can know what the state of their learning is. Also, if students are put in the position of being required to think through and express their ideas, they will be furthering their ability to take control of their learning and use it in other situations (Pimm 1987; Mercer 2000).

Change in the locus of control

At the beginning of the project, the teachers described the changes on which they were embarking as 'scary' – they felt they were being asked to 'give up control' of their classes. We have already mentioned in this chapter reports from several teachers describing this fear. However, towards the end of the project, they talked of the same changes as 'sharing responsibility' with the learners. Students were given more control in the lessons, over what they needed to learn in a topic, how long they would spend on the topic and what activities were engaged in to aid the learning.

> Was all the effort worth it? *Yes* it was. I enjoyed classroom teaching again and although I ended the day tired, I was calm. I was not facing piles of marking. I was looking forward to being creative and to planning the next day. This made me far more positive in my approach to my teaching, I was focusing on the girls' understanding and not on their behaviour. I often found that once the understanding was there the behaviour followed.
>
> (Gwen, Waterford School)

Often a real element of choice was built into the lessons so that students who had reflected on their learning needs could choose their way forward. The teacher was 'the professional' – that is, the one who knew the way through the content, the one who prescribed what was to be learned and the one with the armoury of ideas of ways to help the students learn. The teacher maintained overall control in the lesson but, by sharing the responsibility on issues on which the students could be expected to have a view, some of the big issues of 'controlling' a class were ameliorated. As Robert, at Two Bishops School, said, 'What formative assessment has done for me is made me focus less on myself but more on the children. I have had to have the confidence to empower the students to take it forward'. Making it possible for the students to take more responsibility for their learning makes them act more responsibly.

Expecting the students to be successful learners and offering them activities and time to become successful learners enhances their self-esteem and encourages them to want to learn more. Responding to each student's voice and attempting to meet their learning needs makes the students see their learning as valuable and something worth spending time on. The students learn a skill that will be important to them throughout their lives. This is a feature of great importance, for any exploration of the ways in which society is likely to change in the future is bound to point to the overwhelming importance of the capability to learn anew, and then re-learn, as rapid changes overtake us.

Changes in the role of students

The changes in the teachers' expectations of their students meant that students had to change their role in the classroom. In particular, they changed from passive recipients of the knowledge offered by the teacher to active learners who were able to, and were expected to, take responsibility for and manage their own learning. The students were expected to think, to assess themselves, to accept challenging expectations and be collaborative learners.

When students do take some responsibility for their learning – when, in the psychological jargon, they develop the skills of metacognition (thinking about their thinking) – there can be surprising consequences. One of the teachers recounted an incident that occurred during a year 8 science lesson during a hot afternoon. The teacher was aware that the lesson was not going well, with very little response from the students, and he couldn't think of a way to change course. Then one student put up his hand and said, 'Sir, this isn't working is it?' The teacher reported that his first reaction was hostility – he felt that the student was criticizing him. But after a moment's reflection he realized that the student genuinely wanted to help the class's learning and was making a productive contribution to the lesson. The teacher then said, 'You're right. What shall we do?' and there followed a productive discussion about ways to take the learning forward. Students often have profound insights into their own learning, which can be developed further through formative assessment. Trying to teach without taking advantage of the insights of the learner makes the task much more difficult, if not impossible.

Some of the teachers found that high-attaining students took to these new roles well, although, as Barbara found, students who are used to just 'getting the answers' may resist such changes. Many students recognize that being active in the learning process means that they will maximize their learning potential and success in their school career. They welcome the opportunities afforded by their new role in the classroom. However, students who have grown used to being tacit observers or 'sleepy onlookers' may well resent having to work harder, especially when such passive learning roles are the norm in other subjects. One teacher was accused by her students of not doing her job because she refused to dictate notes. Another teacher, who in all his other classes managed to introduce formative assessment successfully, had a year 10 class that would not become involved in their learning. They had taken a passive role for so long that he said it was impossible to change their attitude to learning.

Therefore, the period during which the role of the students changes needs to be handled carefully and the students have to be supported as they learn to become active, responsible learners. This requires time and teachers may feel that they do not have this time. However, the KMOFAP teachers felt that time spent helping their students understand the new role they were expected to take was time well spent.

Risks and rewards

The process of change instigated by this project was not one of providing recipes that work. We did not say, 'teach in this way and you will raise standards', but rather, 'think about these ideas, what changes do you see them making to the way you act in the classroom?' The enormous changes in practice that we see now are the result of learning together. We do not think such wholesale and lasting changes would have occurred if we had been able to provide recipes for successful lessons. The changes in beliefs and values are the result of the teachers casting themselves as learners and working with us to learn more.

As we have seen, there is an element of risk involved for both teachers and students, and both, as Roger has described, have to work harder, at least to begin with. Teachers taking on formative assessment are giving their students a voice and in many cases acting so as to make that voice louder. For many teachers that is a difficult road. Control is a big issue in the classroom and teachers, quite rightly, worry about this. Making changes in practice can make a confident teacher feel incompetent. They are setting up an unfamiliar classroom culture and both teacher and students may feel insecure at the start. Teachers have to find their own ways through these problems. However, the KMOFAP teachers also described how empowering their students to learn for themselves made the teacher's job much more personally rewarding.

The changes that follow from working at improving their formative assessment also result in changes in teachers' perception of their role as a teacher. It would be too simplistic to say that teachers who focus on formative assessment see themselves as facilitators and shun the role of dictator (even though, in fact, they do!). A teacher takes on the role of facilitator, coach, lecturer, scaffolder, group animator, orchestral conductor or any other role that is needed to enable their students to learn as well as they can. It is misleading to say that formative assessment requires a teacher to act in a closely defined way. However, it does demand that the motivation that makes a teacher act in a given way is always to involve the students in the learning and to allow the students to be aware of their learning successes.

Each of the teachers on the KMOFAP project changed their beliefs about classroom practice. For example, Derek became highly skilled at evoking from students responses that would show him the students' ideas about a topic, and Ceri has trained her students to tell her what she needs to know in order to help. Katrina has become convinced of the benefits of using clear criteria, partly to clarify the learning objectives, but also to place the students more in control of their learning. And Roger changed from 'a presenter of knowledge' to seeing himself engaged in a partnership of mutual respect and trust where everyone had responsibility for the learning going on. Barbara began to open up the learning process and thereby empowered her students to take control of their own learning. These changes happened when teachers who were already competent practitioners reflected on the ideas that are contained elsewhere in this book and decided, with our support and that of their peers, that they had to make changes. These changes matter. Formative assessment is not an 'add-on' process – if a teacher does not believe that it is right that students are involved in and responsible for their own learning, then any changes made will be superficial and probably short-lived. However, until a teacher begins to act in a way that involves the students in their learning and allows them to articulate their learning needs, the teacher will not discover how empowering this way of acting is.

> Being part of this project has made me look very hard at my teaching and to have the confidence to work in the way that I most enjoyed and not in the way that had been prescribed for me.
>
> (Gwen, Waterford School)

7 Management and support

Marginal or revolutionary?

Changes in teaching cover a spectrum from the marginal, such as the supplementation of the chalkboard by the overhead projector or the interactive white-board, to the radical, such as the introduction of records of achievement for all students and across the whole school. A decision to initiate change to improve the practices of formative assessment might, in intention and in foresight, be located anywhere along this spectrum. This location makes a great deal of difference to the actions taken.

At the marginal end of the spectrum, a small group, or even an individual teacher, might take full responsibility: they will have to seek a minimal level of indulgence (e.g. for students to mark their school tests using peer assessment in groups). If they achieve success for themselves, they might subsequently be able to influence colleagues. Their chances of making a long-lasting change across the school will be small as long as their voluntary efforts are competing with the pressures on their colleagues of mandatory work.

At the other end of the spectrum, a formative assessment project could be taken on and planned as a major change across the whole school and given high priority for initiation and support. Then, all teachers will be involved and any such plan will be so fashioned as to institutionalize the outcomes to secure a lasting change. This approach might involve sudden full-scale adoption by all, but such a sudden change, which would probably be seen as a bureaucratic imposition, is unlikely to be successful. A more reasonable alternative would be a plan that started with limited experiments designed to inform and to lead to growth over several years. Clearly, the implications for management and support are dependent on the location on this spectrum of any commitment to develop formative assessment.

In this chapter, while we draw on the experience of the project schools, we also use a wider range of sources, both from the literature and from the many local education authorities (LEAs) with which we worked. One reason for this is that the context of innovation and support for the project's work in schools was unique to the project, so that our work in Oxfordshire and Medway cannot on its own be a model for others. Another reason is that the project aimed only to provide the basis for wider implementation, both within and between schools: we were not in a position to gather substantial data on the progress of this implementation after our work had finished. One outstanding but hardly surprising lesson from the project schools was the wide variety of types and levels of support experienced by the teachers, ranging from one or two who were 'lone rangers' with very little support to others who could work as a team within their schools and were encouraged to be a resource of influence for their colleagues. Thus, while what follows here may sound like a set of prescriptions, the ideas should be used as starting points for adaptation to contexts rather than for mechanical imitation.

Innovation for the whole school

For most of this chapter, it will be assumed that it is a major change that is intended. There are several justifications for this approach. One justification is that the changes cannot be worth the effort if they are to be kept within the bounds of marginal change: the whole business of classroom learning will have to be transformed if students are to be more actively involved in discussion through better questioning, through peer- and self-assessment, and through involvement in the setting and marking of tests. Changing students' expectations of learning in one year with one or two teachers only, and then expecting them to revert to more passive roles subsequently, will be confusing and unfair to them. At the same time, while school procedures for such practices as marking or the conduct of school tests might have to vary from one class period to the next during a phase of experimental innovation, the full potential for improvement can only be realized when students experience new ways of working consistently across all their classes. Finally, the pressure on the few brave innovators will also be unreasonable and, indeed, they might be well advised not to make the attempt if full-scale support cannot be secured.

A much stronger justification follows from the nature of formative assessment itself. Its development addresses matters that are at the heart of the improvement of teaching and learning, and in this we claim it is filling a vacuum. To explain this claim, consider the following findings from recent studies of the changes in schools. The first is from a study of target setting in some schools in England:

> In none of the nine schools I visited had there been a decision to use targets in order to shift classroom practice and a school's ethos away

from didacticism and pupils' dependence on teachers, towards pupils' greater involvement in setting and assessment of the tasks for themselves or in negotiation with their teachers.

(Blanchard 2002, p. 119)

The second is from an intensive study of changes, over a period of 3 years, in a set of eighty primary and secondary schools in Scotland. Commenting on the lack of focus on learning issues highlighted in their work with primary schools, the authors wrote:

> While there was a great deal of talk about the importance of effective teaching and learning, very few teachers mentioned the nurturing of effective learners as part of their school goals and vision.
>
> (Robertson and Toal 2001, p. 113)

Matters were much the same in the secondary schools:

> In secondary schools, it was more common for staff to stress academic outcomes rather than the process of learning itself. There was markedly less emphasis on developing learners except when it came to discussion of personal and social development.
>
> (Robertson and Toal 2001, p. 114)

For most of the last 15 years, the approach to reform in schools has appeared to focus on almost every aspect of their work except the one that lies at the heart of their task – the conduct of learning and teaching in the classroom. In addressing this core aspect directly, the work of formative assessment is bound to be radical in its effects. One school experienced the effects in terms of the changes in the roles of students:

> I want them to think about what they are doing and what they want to do to improve their learning. I don't think we can just give them information and they just soak it up and regurgitate it later. I want the kids to ask questions about why they are doing something, about how is the best way to do it, and I think that stems from the kind of questioning that they are doing as part of the project . . . I think that self-assessment has helped, it has actually helped in many ways. The kids now know the criteria – what is right and what is wrong. And also peer assessment is a major change.
>
> (Deputy head, Waterford School)

As has emerged in previous chapters, what might seem at first sight merely as a set of changes in methods, can in fact produce profound changes in the role of students as learners and in the role of teachers in developing students' capacity to learn. Our experience shows that such changes can enhance the confidence and fulfilment of both teachers and students and can raise standards of test performance. There is, therefore, a strong case for any school to consider seriously the target of securing these benefits right across the school in such a way that they become a permanent part of the culture of the school.

A strategy for change

Teachers need motivation and justification if they are expected to take on the burdens of change. Few of the changes introduced for school improvement have such compelling research evidence in their support as does formative assessment. It can be important to stress this evidence at the outset because external pressures have forced many teachers to focus narrowly on producing better test results rather than more broadly on improving the quality of learning. So it is important that staff are aware that the development of formative assessment is much more than 'this year's new idea'.

In this section, the various components of a plan for change are set out. The first step is to have a clear and ambitious vision of the *aims* of the strategy. Then an audit of *existing strengths* in formative work can provide a starting point for *implementation* of a concrete plan. Features requiring attention in any plan are provision of *support* for those involved and ongoing *evaluation* and *dissemination*. Finally, the plan must be framed within an overall *timetable* for its implementation.

The development plan for the KMOFAP project, as outlined in Chapter 3, is relevant here. However, while reference will be made to this experience, that project cannot provide a ready-made template – although it is possible to build on the project's findings, schools cannot have the level of investment and support that was available for the KMOFAP work.

Aims and vision

Given a radical commitment to transformation of learning through formative assessment, any overall plan should be formulated in the light of this commitment. The core of such a plan will be a vision. The vision will be that students' involvement in their own learning will be enhanced in all of their learning work in the school, that they will come to understand and accept a fundamental change in their role as responsible learners, and that all will become confident that they can achieve progress in learning by their own efforts. A deputy head in one of the project schools looked to the future in these terms:

> [It's essential] that we have a greater emphasis on children's learning, that we are supporting learning far more than we are doing at the moment. I don't think that we do it particularly well. Individuals do, but I don't think that we are using our assessment to progress learning. It doesn't happen overnight. So if you are saying 'what do I want in five years time?' – ideally it's that all staff are using assessment as a tool to develop children's learning.
>
> (Deputy head, Century Island School)

This vision will imply corresponding changes in the role of the teachers, in their perception of the nature of their task and in their confidence in their capacity to implement change in their own way and in their own practice. The implications, for different individual teachers and in different departments, will be diverse and the implementation of the plan should be seen as a voyage of discovery, with the risk and challenge that such a voyage implies. In particular, the possibility of failures and of crises *en route* has to be anticipated.

Such 'vision talk' might seem to some to be naively romantic, using vague rhetoric to lead one away from the realities. So it has to be accompanied by explicit activities; that is, the practical actions that will be pursued to achieve the vision have to be understood and built into a concrete plan of actions. Here, the detailed activities set out in Chapter 4 provide the basic menu. What has to be decided is a sequence and a time frame, appropriate to the school, for implanting and then spreading the practices.

However whole-hearted and ambitious the approach, support from heads of department and the senior school management ought to be secured, and be given after careful consideration. Teachers who are keen to try changes should not invest effort under conditions that are unfavourable. Furthermore, extra efforts by such teachers are a potentially valuable resource for their school: senior staff should plan to explore such potential even if, at the outset, they might not be sure that the innovation has a central part to play in a school's development plan.

Start from strengths

Whatever the type of plan that is fashioned, it should start with a review and audit of existing practice designed to address such questions as

- What are the existing strengths of the school in promoting students' learning?
- How can we find out what these are?
- How can a plan build on them?
- In what respects are the staff close to, or a long way from, the practices that should be encouraged?

- Does this school's existing priorities and plans value students' learning as a top priority – or has this obviously central priority been lost sight of in the pursuit of more marginal goals?

Thus, the first activity proposed for the teachers at the first INSET of the KMOFAP project was to audit their own practices and report back on their findings to the second INSET. Although this exposed the variety and also some important differences in understanding of the ideas, it also served to recognize existing professional expertise and to avoid raising unnecessary fears of radical de-skilling.

Implementation

The larger vision implies an aim of securing a radical change in the practices of teaching and learning throughout the whole school. However, even with such an aim, it could still be argued that a plan for implementation should start on a small scale with a few groups. One reason for this is that no 'recipes' from work elsewhere can constitute an optimum, or even a feasible, plan for any particular school – the history, the culture, the style of management, and the particular strengths and weaknesses of any school interlink to constitute its unique ecology: any change has to be moulded by adaptation if it is to survive in, let alone enrich, that ecology. Nevertheless, the KMOFAP experiences as outlined in Chapters 4, 5 and 6 are an important resource for getting teachers started. Althought these were developed in only three subjects, extension to other subjects have been explored in these and in other schools (for more details, see Chapter 5).

However, it is almost inevitable that, while some teachers might be receptive to the ideas and arguments for change, others might be resistant or nervous and might only be won over by the example of colleagues and by evidence of the responses of the students whom they have to teach. While such an argument might apply to any change affecting the work of teachers, it applies with particular force to the changes discussed in this book, for they are intimate in the sense that they involve the core of a teacher's work with students in their classroom. 'One size fits all' cannot apply at this level – each teacher has to fashion their own way of implementing these changes – no bureaucratic imposition can secure such implementation. The experiences of our project, discussed in Chapter 6, have shown that while different teachers might all incorporate new practices into their teaching, they will differ from one another in their trajectories of change, both in time scale and in the priority they give to different methods and approaches.

> . . . there hasn't been anybody who said 'it's a complete waste of time, I ain't doing that!' So they are all taking up bits and pieces of it, not

necessarily all of it but they are trying bits and pieces . . . even our less enthusiastic teachers are saying, 'Ah that was quite good'. 'I tried that.' 'Oh I tried that and that worked'. Almost 'What a surprise it worked!' 'I thought it was a complete lot of old cods and you know', ... I made a decision that we weren't going to say we are going to have formative assessment, we are going to do this – because people say 'Oh yeah! You're going to tell me what to do". What we have done is a softly softly approach, and I think it is being successful in that we have done some presentations and staff have said 'Oh that is quite good, I am quite interested in that'.

(Deputy head, Century Island School)

One way to start might be to select two departments that will be helped to implement the ideas over one school year, with each teacher starting by select-ing only one of the activities, and then, after a few months and by study of the experience of colleagues, expanding their repertoire by adding others. At the end of the school year, the innovators might produce a report, including evaluation of their work, for all to study. This might lead, in the next year, to further development in their own departments while other selected depart-ments, perhaps all, might set out on the first stage. However, as one deputy head decided, heads of department might be too busy to sustain such a development:

I thought it was important to feed back to heads of departments and they can talk to their departments about it. But then as a result of that what we decided to do was to set up an assessment group. So we asked for representatives from each department to come to a group so that they could hear more about the project information and then go and try some of the ideas.

(Deputy head, Waterford School)

Thus, an alternative plan might be to have a small group of teachers from different departments constitute the first trial group, so that subsequent dis-semination would be within departments as well as across them. A third alter-native would be to initiate the changes across the whole of one year group, on the grounds that this would be a more valid way of focusing and evaluating the innovation on changing the perceptions and practices of students: a dif-ficulty with this approach is that all teachers in the group have to take part whether or not they are committed to the success of the approach.

The approaches outlined above make clear the choice that has to be made between single departmental groups or cross-departmental groups for trying out the first stages of an innovation. The former might appear to have obvious advantages. However, once teachers get beyond a view that their own subject faces unique difficulties, they can pick up ideas from other subjects that can be adapted for their own subject (the idea of traffic lights was introduced to our project by a history teacher). Whatever choice is made, all will recognize that there are specific differences between subjects. As one deputy head, discussing dissemination across the school, foresaw:

> I can see that it could quite possibly transform some departments, and it would be interesting to know how it can affect others. Modern languages, I see might be a difficult issue. But I think the arts . . . might be entirely different and very interesting and exciting . . . I suspect their way of working . . . could be quite closely identified as formative assessment.
>
> (Deputy head, Cornbury Estate School)

Supporting innovation

It is essential that senior management set up a system to support those who are pioneers in the innovation. The first essential step in the KMOFAP work was for the project leaders to meet with the LEA officer and the head of each of the selected schools to clarify what would be involved and to ensure that the teachers would be supported. A plan of support has to be based on an understanding of the purpose of the concrete actions that it will involve. In any such plan, certain essential conditions would have to be built in. Some elements of a system of support can be set out as follows:

- Initial support provided, for example, by an initial INSET in which training can be provided, to those teachers who will be the first to implement the innovations, by those outside the school who have experience and expertise.
- Where possible support from one key individual who acts as a 'critical friend' – this could be achieved by colleagues supporting one another, or possibly by someone from outside, for example from the LEA.
- Time for regular sharing of experiences with colleagues and opportunities perhaps, with outside stimulus, to reflect on immediate experiences in the light of the overall vision, which would involve giving time to the issues discussed in Chapter 5.
- Overt support from a member of the school management team who knows at least something about formative assessment and is keen to find out more.
- Release from any school policies that might inhibit particular innovations.
- Consultation with parents so that they will understand the effects on their children.

- A timetable for the innovation, allowing for a slow build-up in the initial stages.
- Plans for the sharing and diffusion of the ideas as experience is developed.
- An explicit commitment to the innovation in the school's priorities by inclusion in the school's development plan.
- At the outset, similar, perhaps less intensive, INSET for the whole school, so that all colleagues not initially involved can understand the vision and the content of the plan and can be made aware of the strength of the evidence that the developments proposed can be effective.
- Opportunities for visits to, or by experienced teachers from, other schools.

With the exception of the last two, all of these ideas were used in our project, either as part of the work of the King's team or by the LEAs or schools themselves. Several of them call for further discussion. For the initial stages, the stimulus coming from any outside source or agency ought to include an emphasis on its limited status – that is, that there is no 'package' that can be simply be copied into existing practice. Then the work of any group of innovators might proceed as follows. To start with, it might be useful to explore the use of some simple techniques (such as 'traffic lighting') that could be implemented in a straightforward way – this has been shown to be important in getting teachers started.

> ... what was really great about the King's project was they would come back from the sessions and there would be something they would try right now ... this was proper action based research and not 'go thou and get thy whole faculty to do it or go thou and get the whole school to do it'. They would come back, start trying out their traffic lights or whatever it would be, Nancy and Tom would talk to each other about it – that would then of course involve an informal faculty dialogue.
>
> (Deputy head, Riverside School)

Several of our teachers used the research officers as 'critical friends' in supporting a process of change (Doherty *et al.* 2001). A critical friend is a person, usually from outside the school, with relevant experience and expertise, who acts as a confidential 'sounding board' without taking on the role of director and evaluator. The role is to work for the success of the innovation through both support and challenge to those involved, so that they can be helped to reflect on both purposes and processes as a programme develops and can also learn to evaluate themselves. However, colleagues within school can play a similar role, providing reciprocal support and challenge for one another within a community of others who are developing their work on formative assessment.

The LEA may, through the adviser or officer with responsibility for leading the development, offer a potential 'critical friend' to the schools involved. In this way, the developing expertise of the teachers can be valued so that they, the school's management and other schools throughout the LEA recognize the importance of the work they are doing. Within their schools, this often has the effect of heightening awareness of the need to facilitate the development work by providing time for the teachers involved to collaborate, and time and opportunity for disseminating to the other members of staff. It often results in the work being seen as sufficiently significant both to be regularly evaluated at senior management level and reported to governors.

When several have tried a few ideas between them, one member of the group might introduce the technique that she or he has tried out, and then the other members of the group have to find a way that the technique could be used in their own teaching. This not only generates a large number of techniques that can then be tried out, but by seeing how each technique is adapted all of the group can come to recognize the salience and purpose of that technique and to understand its formative potential. For all of these initiatives, it is essential to keep the formative use in the forefront: a new practice might help collect better information about students' thinking, but if it stops short of using, or of showing students how to use, that information to improve each student's learning, it misses the whole point of the exercise.

It should be clear from this account that provision of time for teachers engaged in trying new practices to discuss their experiences with colleagues, and to hear of other teachers' experiences with similar experiences, is a crucial part of the stimulus for sustaining the process of change.

> The 'one person going out' model doesn't work if . . . the rest of the people in the school don't have the time to listen when he gets back. As I say working within the department . . . I think that has worked well . . . it's wonderful at a departmental meeting to have a slot where you actually talk about teaching and learning and you know you're not talking about how you're going to administer the next lot of exams or making sure the chairs are stacked at the end of the day.
>
> (Deputy head, Cornbury Estate School)

As described in Chapter 3, the meetings of our project teachers, originally organized by us, were increasingly taken over by them, both in terms of what was discussed and, later, even in the running of the meetings. The lesson that we learned is that any leaders or managers should support and welcome such a shift – the initial stimulus might come from the top, but the playing out of the action has to be the responsibility of those on the ground. The support needed at this stage is of validation – that is, recognition that such an exchange of ideas, which can often seem little more than a sharing of anecdotes, is not only an acceptable use of teachers' time, but is actually to be encouraged. There are advantages in that discussion between teachers, and particularly between teachers of different subjects, can help all to 'think out of their box': different departments interpret ideas differently, so that comparisons between existing practices and between experiences with innovations can help open up new and creative ideas.

A further essential is the creation of more structured opportunities for reflection. The King's team found that the teachers were sometimes unaware of the cumulative effect of the changes they had made during the project and recommended that each should keep a record of their work in a journal. These journals helped them think about weaving together the various techniques into more coherent strategies, but also provided vivid accounts of the work that could be used to encourage other teachers to develop their practice along the same lines. While writing journals will not be appropriate for all settings, it will be important to structure teachers' reflections in some way – after all, simply asking teachers to reflect on their experience is unlikely to be productive. One useful technique is for groups of teachers to 'unpack' actions that are normally undertaken without time for thinking. For example, a group of teachers can profitably spend an hour discussing how to mark half-a-dozen students' books, exploring the assumptions that need to be made about where each student has reached, about what would be appropriate 'next steps' and about communicating the advice through written comments.

Another issue is the release from the constraints of some school policies. In framing their 'action plans' for what they wanted to change in their practice, many of the teachers in our project felt constrained by school policies on assessment. For example, while reducing the salience of grades and marks (or abandoning their use completely for classwork and homework) was felt to be desirable by most teachers, they believed that this would not be allowed by the senior management of their schools. Only a quarter of the teachers (6 of 24) included comment-only marking in their initial action plans, and although many more (18 of 24) had moved towards comment-only marking of classwork and homework by the end of the project, it is clear that school policies acted to constrain innovation. School leaders have a role in not merely allowing such innovations, but also in creating an environment in which teachers' ideas about how to improve things are actively encouraged and valued.

A further aspect in planning for support is to consider provision of any necessary resources. In the present case, the physical resources are minimal, although such matters as the layout of classrooms to make group work possible, and the provision of means to make it easy for different individuals or groups to share and to display work, might need attention. The essential and most difficult resource is the time, both of management and of teachers involved. The importance of planning and discussion time has already been stressed. The nettle that will have to be grasped is that teachers do not have chunks of spare time waiting to be used up. In other words, something has got to go – that is, some activity judged to be less important than the new initiative has to be abandoned by those who will need new free time to pursue the innovation. The importance of a comprehensive plan is that it can highlight the need for such hard decisions, and also help decide on a reduction in existing loads for particular individuals on the grounds that they need the time to make a new contribution to the improvement of the school as a whole.

Evaluation

Given that the first innovators are to help build the capacity of the school to implement the plan, evaluation of their efforts is essential, so that occasions for reviewing progress and for the modification of plans in the light of experience must be built in from the outset. Such reviews must be informed by the collection of evaluation evidence. Here it is necessary to be clear about what is being evaluated and, thereby, sustained and improved. In particular, it will be helpful to attend to the two aspects of the process and the content of innovation. The process is the work of initiation, of follow-up meetings, of opportunities for discussion and reflection and, as explored further below, of evaluation and dissemination. The content is the actual classroom activity and the associated work, particularly with homework. Progress in these aspects involves such issues as the quality of questioning and classroom dialogue, the quality of comments on homework and of students' use of these, and the development among students of peer- and self-assessment.

Such evaluation should not be left to the innovators themselves – it should be pre-planned so that pre- and post-collection of data can give evidence of changes. One aspect would be the collection and analysis of test data along the lines discussed in the last section of Chapter 3. Another would be the formulation and application of questionnaires to students about their perceptions of the classrooms in which changes are being implemented, perhaps involving comparisons, using the same questionnaires, with other classrooms. A third source would be reports, preferably in written form based upon their journals, from the teachers involved recording their experiences, both of the classroom work and of the support received.

The aspect of evaluation might be further developed in the light of the need to sustain progress well beyond a first experimental year. Progress of any change programme might by helped by setting and checking on targets. Suitable targets could be devised in relation to learning and teaching practices. Examples might be:

- at least some questions asked in a class should be followed by ample wait time and lead to involvement of many students in subsequent discussion;
- homework books should show comments together with evidence that students have acted on these comments to subsequently improve their work;
- discussion in groups involving peer-assessment of one another's work should be a regular feature in classrooms.

The achievement of such targets might well be checked by peer-assessment among teachers through observations in one another's class-rooms. Such observations should be opportunities for mutual feedback and not be seen as 'inspections'. Indeed, the work with and between teachers should mirror the practices and attitudes that they are trying to establish for their students: in their work with one another, teachers should reflect the practices that should be developed with their students, including where necessary a shift from competition and judgement to collaboration and for-mative feedback.

The timetable and dissemination

In setting a timetable, it should be noted that the experience of the KMOFAP work was that, although the classrooms of most of the teachers involved in the project were changed radically, this change was gradual and slow. Half-way through the project, (i.e. after a year), many of the teachers had changed only small details in their practice and although these changes were significant changes for them, the outward appearance was that little had changed. For some, it might have been tempting at this point to have concluded that the intervention was not working and that something else needed to be done. However, during the second half of the project, the changes became much more radical and, for many of the teachers, the various techniques that they had adopted cohered to form a unified approach to formative assessment. Of course, schools taking on the developments described in this book will start with the advantage of the experiences and insights reported and discussed here, so that they might be able to develop practices more rapidly. So we cannot predict how long it might take for changes to 'take off'.

Our best estimate is that initial experiences and evidence of outcomes ought to provide some useful evidence after about a year of work and, on this basis, adoption by the whole school might be envisaged in a second year, or might be further phased-in over two more years. The overall purpose of the evaluation plans should be to secure for the school, from the first stages of innovation, evidence that might inform subsequent decisions about the development and diffusion of changes across the school.

It is not possible to give further advice here on what the next steps in dissemination should be, for these would clearly depend on the plan adopted for the initial stage of innovation, on the ways in which that stage had been supported and on the lessons learned from its evaluation. What is obvious is that those directly involved in any first stage will be a valuable resource for their colleagues in the further development, that any initial plan will have to be flexible in the light of experience as it accumulates, and in particular that the support needed for such further development needs to be reviewed as evidence of progress and pitfalls emerges.

Sustainability has in the past been the Achilles heel of many innovations, not least because, after (say) a year, another idea comes along and the temptation to adopt it seems too strong to resist. What matters here are both the depth of conviction underlying the initial commitment and a realism that without sustained concentration and support, any plan for change will yield poor returns and, while it might enrich a few individuals, will not achieve the permanent improvement that would justify the school's investment.

> If anything is going to happen it has to feature on agendas, so I have asked heads of faculty when the minutes come in, can you put formative, is it on there? . . . There is if you like the uncomfortable part of trying something new – being prepared to think about the lesson, what sorts of questions you are going to ask – and in order to do that people have got to feel this is worth doing . . . If you are going to do this, well let's come back, let's learn from each other, let's report back. That's why I think unless you put it on agendas, and ask people to put it on, it will be diluted.
>
> (Deputy head, Two Bishops School)

Leadership, stimulus and support

From the top

Any decision to embark on a programme for the improvement of learning and teaching in a school will only lead to a sustained change in the school's work if it has at the outset, or comes to have as it develops, full support from the leadership, be it individual in a headteacher or collective in the school leadership. The first step in taking any such decision is to be clear about the priority to be given to the initiative: it should not be marginalized by a further new initiative before there has been adequate time for the new style of working to be firmly established. In addition to a choice from the top for sustained commitment, there should also be a coherent and productive resonance with previous priorities that have bedded in as part of the school's work.

Given a choice, the task of leadership is to set the agenda, win commitment to that agenda and motivate staff to work to it. One study of change leadership has identified two key ingredients:

> It is our contention that how effectively planning is undertaken depends to a significant extent on how well the change leaders in the school understand the content and process of change. This understanding is often the outcome of their own motivation, and the resulting combination of developed expertise and commitment gives effective change leaders the impetus to use more powerful and persistent approaches to change and to maintain a strategic focus. Simple operationalization of initiatives which are neither fully understood by change leaders nor personally engaging to them results in superficial change which has little real impact on the school.
>
> (Reeves *et al.* 2001, p. 136)

For the aspect of content, there has to be a clear vision. For formative assessment, as emphasized earlier, that has to be a vision about the basic focus on the learning of the students as developed through their activities and their developing roles as learners in the classroom. There also has to be some depth of understanding of what is actually involved in practice. The study quoted above concluded by pointing to evidence from work both in schools and in the commercial sector that the leaders who make a difference are those who 'engage and invest intellectually as well as emotionally in the purpose and nature of their business' (Reeves *et al.* 2001, p. 136).

For the aspect of process, most of the components for a plan of action were spelt out in the previous section of this chapter. All that is important here is that there ought to be a sustained plan with a time horizon of at least 2 years, with persistence in initiation, support, evaluation and review. According to the size of the school, specific tasks may have to be assigned. The management of the process may not necessarily lie in the same hands as leadership in vision and content. Where the task of 'assessment coordinator' is specified, it ought to be made clear whether this involves responsibility for the content, for the process or for both dimensions of innovation in assessment, and it is important to be clear that this task is at the heart of learning in the school and not to be confused with the administration of examinations.

At departmental level

In a secondary school, the head of department is usually a key figure in any change process, for he or she is the link between the individual teacher and the school policy as articulated by the leadership. Most plans will depend for their implementation on the work of individual departments. If their task is to promote changes in the way teachers work in their classrooms, heads of department cannot work effectively if they are merely passing on orders rather than committing themselves to full personal support (Dillon 2000, p. 127): their capacity to make sense of changes with their departmental colleagues is a crucial resource. To serve this purpose, the head of department must make time and space for the staff to discuss the change initiative. Discussion among colleagues is essential for clarifying understandings of the purposes and practices involved, for ensuring a context of collegial support as individual teachers take on the risks of changing their classroom practice, for promoting reflection on the issues raised and in providing the forum for evaluation. This may be summed up by pointing out that teachers need the support and benefits of peer-assessments as much as their students do. The departmental discussion ought to be the place where leadership, collaboration, communication and a focus on learning and teaching come together to foster improvements for every teacher. In so far as these characteristics have been or are being developed, so will the department and the school strengthen their capacity for change.

From outside the school

Various outside agencies can support the institutional development of a school and the professional development of its teachers. The contribution of the local education authority can be particularly valuable. The LEA can provide access to expertise and experience, from other schools, from the resources of its own officers and from links with research and consultancy agencies. These it can call upon to give support at critical stages, notably in stimulating the initial commitment and the formulation of a programme, in giving feedback throughout the process to catalyse progress, and in help with ongoing evaluation.

Local education authorities can help to support development work of this kind in a few schools, but they can also help to ensure that successes are widely published within the authority and that as many schools as possible are able to learn from the developing expertise of the teachers involved. Dissemination should therefore be a high priority at LEA level. In some LEAs, where the benefits of the introduction of formative assessment strategies have been fully recognized, a commitment to developing teacher expertise in this area is central to the LEA's school improvement work. It is helpful if this can be reflected in its education development plan and, consequently, in the resources provided for development work in terms of personnel time to support it. This can ensure that the work is given a high profile and that such existing networks as headteacher forums, subject networks and national strategy consultant groups are expected to reflect on the key features of the success of the formative assessment work and build on these.

Local education authorities can also help by setting up networks through which schools embarking on the same venture can keep in touch with one another, both at the level of senior management and at the level of subject departments. A valuable extension of this idea is to create a formative assessment network for schools in the LEA not yet involved but committed to learning more about the initiative and introducing the work in one or more of their departments.

The input of teachers who have already developed their work in formative assessment can be especially valuable to an extension network because of its sound practical basis and because the extension network teachers are able to engage in discussion that helps them to remodel the exemplification offered, in the context of their own situations and their own subject. It also enables both groups to consider and probe the similarities and differences, the possibilities and limitations of formative assessment strategies in different subject contexts. An incidental although considerable benefit for the teachers further advanced in developing formative practice is precisely that which the formative assessment strategy of peer tutoring offers in the classroom: it provides them with opportunities to reflect on their work and consolidate their understanding of the process through coaching other teachers. An LEA that is committed to development across all its schools can, year on year, facilitate the extension of the network, thereby creating a group of mutually supporting teachers in which there is opportunity both to learn and to pass on expertise, the sort of conditions that are widely recognized to be very favourable for professional development. These ideas are reinforced in advice from the Department for Education and Skills (2001):

> CPD activities that have most impact on classroom practice:
>
> - opportunities to learn from and with other teachers, in their own or other schools;
> - by observing colleagues teaching and discussing what they have observed;
> - through collaborative enquiry into real school improvement problems, drawing on best practice in developing solutions;
> - by taking part in coaching or mentoring;
> - high quality focused training on specific skill area, underpinned by excellent teaching materials and direct support to apply their learning back in the classroom.
>
> (DfES 2001)

The LEA is in a unique position to provide one particularly important service to schools. That is, to create a climate in which innovation can be introduced without fear of teachers suffering from 'initiative overload': it can make links across the many demands, strategies, initiatives and projects that schools are expected to consider and/or introduce in the interests of developing their practice. Given that any LEA's key role is to improve learning, it should organize its training and support to link the various initiatives and strategies that will further this aim, including: formative assessment; developing teachers' expertise which is at the heart of the key stage 3 strategy; raising the achievement of boys; the inclusion agenda. All these can be linked within coordinated LEA provision to provide coherence to schools.

Finally, moving outside the context of development within a single LEA, formative assessment expertise can be disseminated on a broader canvas through inter-LEA officer and adviser links, notably the Association for Achievement and Improvement through Assessment (AAIA). Local education authorities keen to encourage their schools to introduce formative assessment strategies use these professional contacts to invite teachers involved in the initiative from outside their authority to present case study material at conferences and training sessions. Often the combination of presentations from university personnel, LEA advisers and teachers provides a powerful catalyst for professional development, bringing together the theoretical basis, the research evidence, the management issues and the practical application.

In addition to LEAs, a range of agencies, whether from universities and colleges, professional associations and even government, can also play a role. What is important is that their influence is such as to acknowledge the limits of any advice or recipes that they might offer, and to recognize that the critical feature in any reform is the way in which the individual teachers can translate the ideas into their personal action within their classrooms.

8 The end – and a beginning

Risky journeys

Any attempt to turn ideas into practice will be a learning experience, but also a risky one. Indeed, practical learning and risk often go together. One risk in our venture was that teachers might have found the tasks that it set them to be unacceptable or impossible. Although they did not decide to refuse or to ignore the challenge, there was still the risk that the changes proposed might have been found feasible but unacceptable. Yet these potential disasters did not happen – so why were the outcomes so positive and so rewarding?

One answer to this question surely lies in the potential of the ideas behind the project. Yet while the positive outcomes may have been due in part to this potential, the professionalism and commitment of the teachers formed a second essential component. The interaction of these two – that is, the power of the ideas to bring out the professionalism and talents of teachers – was clearly a further catalyst for success.

It is useful to analyse more thoroughly this question of the reasons for the success of the project, partly as a way of seeing the work described here from different perspectives, but mainly because such analysis should help those who will draw lessons for their own action from our work. They should find it useful as they anticipate or reflect on their own experiences. So what is attempted in this chapter is an analysis of the lessons that were learned about the enterprise as it unfolded. This will be done in terms of four themes – research into practice, deeper implications, developing the formative concept, and achieving impact.

One might ask, were we smart or were we lucky? This is a question we have often asked ourselves. We can say that much of what is described here in hindsight was in fact learned in the process and was anticipated, if at all, only dimly at the outset. However, the approach in this chapter is not to pass judgement on the reasons for success, but rather to draw lessons from the experience which might be useful to others.

Research into practice

As outlined in Chapter 3, the King's team started with the belief that results of research studies cannot provide ready-made recipes for practice. Even if a research is conducted within the same contexts of schooling and of culture as those of potential users, the exigencies of rigorous research call for controlled conditions unlike those of most daily practice. Our starting position, that on the basis of research results we could only provide stimulus, challenge and support for the work of teachers in inventing new practical knowledge about classroom work, was fully justified in several ways.

Different teachers adopted and adapted different practices, teachers stimulated and challenged one another as they exchanged experiences, and several new approaches, not anticipated from the research literature, arose in and were disseminated across the group of six schools. The spectrum of outcomes and the diversity in trajectories of change, described in Chapters 4, 5 and 6, are evidence of the richness of this approach. Given that each individual teacher has to make the ideas their own, diversity is bound to go with success. This developing diversity went along with a growing ownership by teachers of the ideas and of the project as a whole. One of the clearest signs of ownership was the way in which the conduct of the meetings of the whole group was gradually taken out of our hands. For example, on the first occasion when a new set of teachers joined the group, much of the work of their induction was done by the 'old hands'.

Thus, while research findings did form the essential starting point of the work, the project itself was a research project (i.e. a venture to establish new knowledge), but one of a very different character from those which inspired it in the first place. Some might describe the work as a development project rather than research, or at least R&D biased towards the D. There are two arguments which might support this criticism. We regard both of them as valid in principle, but irrelevant to the work of our project.

One argument would be that in its empirical aspects, the research, when compared with the research studies that inspired it, was not rigorous. The participants were not chosen at random, so that the sample might not be representative of the generality of teachers and schools; the criteria for success, in so far as these were quantitative, were too variable between different teachers and different schools; the choice of controls was too variable and unsystematic; and the classroom conditions for implementing new practices were too variable. We point out, in response, that the context of the project, with schools and teachers prepared to make a commitment to innovation, and with the conditions of learning and of testing which were those in which most school teaching has to be carried out, matched those in which any findings might be applied. Controlling or distorting these conditions to secure uniformity might produce 'rigorous' results, but the outcome would be irrelevant to the realities of school work.

A second type of criticism would be that the work lacked a clear theoretical basis. General ideas about the nature of learning and about the need for learners to take responsibility in their learning were influential, but the main approach was pragmatic in recommending a set of practices that were justified on empirical grounds and by a variety of theoretical principles. These are valid points about the project's lack of theoretical coherence, but on the other hand it was strong in its practical coherence – a point which is explored further in the next section. A coherent theory of formative assessment has not yet been formulated; indeed, the findings of this project will provide new ideas to serve such formulation. In the complex field of educational research, the task of practical implementation of ideas cannot be described simply as the application of previous knowledge: putting ideas into practice usually leads to those ideas being transformed – new knowledge is being created. The distinction between research and development is not helpful here: the two are intertwined. Thus, any theory of formative assessment that draws on the findings of such knowledge will be grounded in the realities of classroom practice and will, therefore, be far more useful to schools than one that is not so grounded. Such arguments can be found in writings about the nature of new knowledge created by technology – it is not merely 'the appliance of science' (Layton 1991) – and, for educational research, in a paper by Hargreaves (1999) entitled 'The knowledge creating school'.

Deeper implications

There are many practices that can be tried out to improve interaction in learning in the classroom, yet, as described in Chapter 4, the project was in the end based on four of these. With hindsight it can be seen that these four satisfy certain conditions. They could all be accepted as *relevant* to good teaching. The changes that each involved could be seen to be *feasible*, albeit difficult for some to implement. They were also *acceptable* in that teachers could take ownership of them because they were consistent with their beliefs and values as teachers.

Furthermore, they were not wholly independent in their practical implications. Obvious examples of this *synergy* were the properties, implicit in all four, of enhanced participation by students, of transfer of responsibility for their learning to students, and of enhanced student awareness of the difference between knowing and understanding. Together with these common features was the fact that, taken together, the four formed an adequately broad list. The development, arising from teachers, about the formative use of summative tests is a good example. The omission of any work on such tests from our initial agenda was not tolerable, because failure to apply the general principles to the business of testing would be an obstacle to coherence in their practice.

The analysis does show that the set of four activities has inherent in it some robust features that help account for its success, principles that were not explicitly recognized at the outset and which may not be obvious on any first description. Equally subtle is the fact, explained in Chapter 5, that the four are consistent with, and help to implement, fundamental principles of good learning, and help enact principles of supporting the commitment and self-esteem of students. It is because of the way that these two types of issues pervaded all activities that the *synergy* happened.

One practical issue is raised by this reflection. In any programme that aims to replicate the process and achieve the gains secured in our project, one basic choice is now available. The first option is to proceed by the same route as taken by us – that is, to start pragmatically by recommending the practical approaches set out in Chapter 4 and to focus on supporting and evaluating their implementation. The discussion of such theoretical ideas as the nature of learning and the role of the teacher in the cognitive and affective development of the learner could come later, perhaps through an exploration of the reasons why these activities were recommended. This sequence may be represented as follows:

Set of activities → their synergy/comprehensiveness → cognitive/affective insights

However, an alternative approach is possible, for given that the implications and links of the activities to more general principles are now understood, one could start an INSET programme from the learning principles and proceed from these to the practical activities, thus reversing the sequence as follows:

Cognitive/affective insights → need for synergy/comprehensiveness → set of activities

We are not in a position to say which would be the best approach, and it may well be that the choice will depend on the context: where the activities are mainly novel, the first of the two sequences might be more appropriate, whereas a need to improve the quality of familiar practices might be better met by the second.

Developing the formative concept

The clarification of the concept of formative assessment has been one of the significant features of our work. To some, it has in the past implied the collection of marks from homework tasks and from class tests, as opposed to marks from formal testing, formative being seen as no more than frequent informal testing (i.e. as 'micro-summative' assessment). For others, 'formative' implies informal, as opposed to testing which is formal, but limited to the purpose of improving learning. Yet formal testing can be used to improve learning and to serve more than one purpose, while informal assessment can be used for summative purposes. The phrase 'assessment for learning' has become a common substitute for 'formative assessment', yet there is also possible ambiguity in this label. Information about learning can be gained from any assessment designed to produce such information, but if this is used for recording purposes or for long-term curriculum improvement, it will not help the learning of the students currently involved. It might be formative for the teacher, but not for the students.

So, as has been made particularly clear in the discussion of feedback in Chapter 4, it is important to emphasize the critical criterion – formative assessment is a process, one in which information about learning is *evoked* and then *used* to modify the teaching and learning activities in which teachers and students are engaged. Insistence on a precise criterion does not imply a restricted range of activities. The evidence can be *evoked* in a wide variety of ways, from the puzzled look on a student's face to analysis of that student's response to a homework task or a question in a formal test, but to identify this process, on its own, as feedback is a serious misunderstanding, albeit a common one. After all, a thermostat which turned out to do no more than measure and record temperature change would quickly be discarded as useless. Feedback can only serve learning if it involves both the *evoking* of evidence and a response to that evidence by *using* it in some way to improve the learning. Such an interaction process may involve a teacher with a student, but might also occur between students in peer-assessment work.

The importance of this clarification has emerged during our work and in subsequent short-term work with a wider range of schools. Clarification is important because the claimed advantages only apply to authentic interpretations. Put simply, anyone who believes that they are implementing good formative practices will expect to see some of the benefits that others claim to have experienced, and this expectation may not be satisfied if they have misunderstood the meaning and are thereby not really adopting the practices.

Achieving impact

Publishing can help achieve impact. The booklet *Inside the Black Box* (Black and Wiliam 1998b) has sold about 40,000 copies in the 5 years since its publication. A more recent booklet, *Working Inside the Black Box* (Black *et al.* 2002), has sold about 20,000 copies within 6 months. It is intriguing to speculate on the reasons for this popular impact. Such properties as the length, the style and the low cost must have contributed, but the central reason must lie in the nature of the message.

The frequent contacts that all the members of the King's team have made, with professional associations, with LEA staff and in LEA workshops, and in the INSET days of individual schools, help us to understand why the message has had an impact. It seems to be a combination of two features. The one is the strength of the evidence, both from research literature and from the experiences of the teachers which form the basis of this book. The other is the congruence of what is proposed with the professional priorities and values of teachers.

Although it would be natural to celebrate such impact, we see two further hurdles to be surmounted. The first hurdle is the location of teachers' formative work in the larger context of assessment and testing. Teachers have responsibilities for summative assessment, to inform decisions about the future study choices by and for students, and more generally for reporting progress within school and to parents. The work described in Chapter 4 has shown some ways to improve the forging of consistency and synergy between formative work and these summative requirements. However, such development cannot go further without including a study of teachers' responsibilities both in certification – that is, in preparing students for such external systems as the GCSE certification and in contributing to the teacher-assessed components of such systems – and in responding to the pressure of accountability driven by key stage tests and certification results. Here teachers and schools have little room for implementing some of the approaches described in Chapter 4; the issue is one for those who formulate educational policy. The problems created by the pressures to 'teach to the test' can inhibit good formative practices. So public policy for external testing ought to be reconsidered with a view to giving better and clearer support to, and to making optimum use of, formative practices. Hitherto policies have not been drawn up with this need in mind. Such considerations lie outside the scope of this book, but we hope that the growing recognition of the value of formative assessment can help stimulate and inform a fresh exploration of these issues. The problems and pressures involved are an important part of the context in which formative assessment might be inhibited or, hopefully, encouraged to develop.

The second hurdle is that to fall in love with the ideas is but a start on the long hard road of commitment to the relationship, one in which the numerous and intimate details have to be worked out both at a personal and at an institutional level. Chapters 6 and 7, respectively, enlarge on these two levels. At both levels, what is central is the thoughtfulness and the clarity that underpins the commitment. This book will have succeeded if it helps teachers and schools to develop such thoughtfulness and clarity and to inspire the commitment.

Glossary of terms and acronyms

Unless otherwise specified, all explanations below relate to England, Wales and Northern Ireland. Scotland has an independent education system.

AAIA Association for Achievement and Improvement through Assessment

APU Assessment of Performance Unit: national government surveys of school performance conducted in the 1980s in several subjects

CAT Cognitive Abilities Test: standardized IQ-type test used by the vast majority of secondary schools in England

CPD Continuous professional development: a generic term not a specific process (see INSET below)

DfEE Department for Education and Employment: previous name of government ministry for England

DfES Department for Education and Skills: current name of government ministry for England

GAIM Graded Assessment in Mathematics: system of 'on-demand' assessments to be taken in sequence over a student's five secondary school years, the aggregate automatically earning a GCSE certificate. Developed and operated in the 1980s and 1990s

GASP Graded Assessment in Science Project: as for GAIM

GCSE General Certificate of Secondary Education: national school leaving certificate taken usually at age 16, tested and awarded in single subjects

ILEA Inner London Education Authority

INSET In-service education and training: a generic term for a variety of courses and programmes for teachers. While the project used the term INSET for the plenary teachers' meetings, it was hardly appropriate to describe these as 'training' (see also CPD)

Key stages Elements of the age-sequence structure of the national curriculum. There are four: key stage 1 (ages 5–7, also known as years 1 and 2), key stage 2 (ages 7–11, also known as years 3–6), key stage 3 (ages 11–14, also known as years 7–9), key stage 4 (ages 14–16, also known as years 10 and 11). National tasks or tests in English, mathematics and science have to be taken at the end of key stages 1, 2 and 3, while GCSE examinations are normally taken at the end of key stage 4

KMOFAP King's, Medway, Oxfordshire Formative Assessment Project

LEA Local education authority: Medway and Oxfordshire were the LEA partners in our project

League tables Published tables showing the results in all end of key stage tests for all schools in England

NFER National Foundation for Educational Research in England and Wales: independent testing agency

OFSTED Office for Standards in Education: government agency responsible for regular inspections of all publicly funded schools in England

QCA Qualifications and Curriculum Authority: national agency set up to advise government on all curriculum and assessment issues and to oversee all public examination procedures (England only)

R&D Research and development

TIMSS Third International Mathematics and Science Study

Teacher Training Agency national agency set up to advise government on courses and qualifications for teacher training, and for overseeing procedures for the formal qualification of teachers (England only)

TGAT Task Group on Assessment and Testing

Years 1 to 11 See key stages above

References

Askew, M. and Wiliam, D. (1995) *Recent Research in Mathematics Education 5–16*. London: HMSO.

Askew, M., Brown, M.L., Rhodes, V., Johnson, D.C. and Wiliam, D. (1997) *Effective Teachers of Numeracy: Final Report*. London: School of Education, King's College.

Assessment Reform Group (2002) *Testing, Motivation and Learning*. Cambridge: Cambridge University Faculty of Education, Assessment Reform Group.

Bachor, D.G. and Anderson, G.O. (1994) Elementary teachers' assessment practices as observed in the province of British Columbia, Canada, *Assessment in Education*, 1(1): 63–93.

Beaton, A.E., Mullis, I.V.S., Martin, M.O., Gonzalez, E.J., Kelly, D.L. and Smith, T.A. (1996) *Mathematics Achievement in the Middle School Years*. Boston, MA: Boston College.

Bergan, J.R., Sladeczek, I.E., Schwarz, R.D. and Smith, A.N. (1991) Effects of a measurement and planning system on kindergartners' cognitive development and educational programming, *American Educational Research Journal*, 28(3): 683–714.

Black, P. (1990) APU Science: the past and the future. *School Science Review*, 72(258): 13–28.

Black, P. (1998) *Testing: Friend or Foe? Theory and Practice of Assessment and Testing*. London: Falmer Press.

Black, P. and Wiliam, D. (1998a) Assessment and classroom learning, *Assessment in Education*, 5(1): 7–71.

Black, P. and Wiliam, D. (1998b) *Inside the Black Box: Raising Standards through Classroom Assessment*. London: School of Education, King's College. See also *Phi Delta Kappan*, 80(2): 139–48.

Black, P., Harrison, C., Lee, C., Marshall, B. and Wiliam, D. (2002) *Working Inside the Black Box: Assessment for Learning in the Classroom*. London: Department of Education and Professional Studies, King's College.

Blanchard, J. (2002) *Teaching and Targets*. London: Routledge/Falmer.

Boulet, M.M., Simard, G. and Demelo, D. (1990) Formative evaluation effects on learning music, *Journal of Educational Research*, 84(2): 119–25.

Broadfoot, P., Osborn, M., Panel, C. and Pollard, A. (1996) Assessment in French primary schools; *The Curriculum Journal*, 7(2): 227–46.

Brousseau, G. (1984) The crucial role of the didactical contract in the analysis and construction of situations in teaching and learning mathematics, in

H.-G. Steiner (ed.) *Theory of Mathematics Education: ICME 5 Topic Area and Miniconference*, pp. 110–19. Bielefeld, Germany: Institut für Didaktik der Mathematik der Universität Bielefeld.

Brown, M. (1989) Graded assessment and learning hierarchies in mathematics: an alternative view, *British Educational Research Journal*, 15(2): 121–8.

Butler, R. (1987) Task-involving and ego-involving properties of evaluation: effects of different feedback conditions on motivational perceptions, interest and performance, *Journal of Educational Psychology*, 79(4): 474–82.

Butler, R. (1988) Enhancing and undermining intrinsic motivation: the effects of task-involving and ego-involving evaluation on interest and performance. *British Journal of Educational Psychology*, 58: 1–14.

Butler, R. and Neuman, O. (1995) Effects of task and ego-achievement goals on help-seeking behaviours and attitudes, *Journal of Educational Psychology*, 87(2): 261–71.

Cavendish, S., Galton, M., Hargreaves, L. and Harlen, W. (1990) *Observing Activities*. London: Paul Chapman.

Claxton, G.L. (1995) What kind of learning does self-assessment drive? Developing a 'nose' for quality: comments on Klenowski, *Assessment in Education*, 2(3): 339–43.

Craven, R.G., Marsh, H.W. and Debus, R.L. (1991) Effects of internally focused feedback on enhancement of academic self-concept, *Journal of Educational Psychology*, 83(1): 17–27.

Dassa, C. (1990) From a horizontal to a vertical method of integrating educational diagnosis with classroom assessment, *The Alberta Journal of Educational Research*, 36(1): 35–44.

Dassa, C., Vazquez-Abad, J. and Ajar, D. (1993) Formative assessment in a classroom setting: from practice to computer innovations, *The Alberta Journal of Educational Research*, 39(1): 111–25.

Daws, N. and Singh, B. (1996) Formative assessment: to what extent is its potential to enhance pupils' science being realised?, *School Science Review*, 77(281): 93–100.

Department for Education and Employment (1998) *The National Literacy Strategy: Framework for Teaching*. London: DfEE.

Department for Education and Employment (2001) *The National Literacy Strategy: Framework for Teaching English: Years 7, 8 and 9*. London DfEE.

Department for Education and Skills (2001) *Learning and Teaching – A Strategy for Professional Development*, DfEE 0071/2001. London: DfES.

Dillon, J. (2000) Managing the science department, in M. Monk and J. Osborne (eds) *Good practice in science teaching: What research has to say*, pp. 123–38. Buckingham: Open University Press.

Doherty, J., MacBeath, J., Jardine, S., Smith, I. and McCall, J. (2001) Do schools need critical friends? in J. Macbeath and P. Mortimore (eds) *Improving School Performance*, pp. 138–51. Buckingham: Open University Press.

Dweck, C.S. (1986) Motivational processes affecting learning, *American Psychologist* (*Special Issue: Psychological Science and Education*), 41(10): 1040–8.

Fairbrother, R., Black, P.J. and Gill, P. (eds) (1994) *Teachers Assessing Pupils: Lessons from Science Classrooms*. Hatfield: Association for Science Education.

Fernandes, M. and Fontana, D. (1996) Changes in control beliefs in Portuguese primary school pupils as a consequence of the employment of self-assessment strategies, *British Journal of Educational Psychology*, 66: 301–13.

Foos, P.W., Mora, J.J. and Tkacz, S. (1994) Student study techniques and the generation effect, *Journal of Educational Psychology*, 86(4): 567–76.

Fuchs, L.S. and Fuchs, D. (1986) Effects of systematic formative evaluation: a meta-analysis, *Exceptional Children*, 53(3): 199–208.

Gipps, C., McCallum, B. and Brown, M. (1997) Models of teacher assessment among primary school teachers in England, *The Curriculum Journal*, 7(2): 167–83.

Grisay, A. (1991) Improving assessment in primary schools: 'APER' research reduces failure rates, in P. Weston (ed.) *Assessment of Pupils' Achievement: Motivation and School Success*, pp. 103–18. Amsterdam: Swets and Zeitlinger.

Hargreaves, D.H. (1999) The knowledge creating school, *British Journal of Educational Studies*, 47(2): 122–44.

King, A. (1992) Facilitating elaborative learning through guided student-generated questioning, *Educational Psychologist*, 27(1): 111–26.

Kluger, A.N. and DeNisi, A. (1996) The effects of feedback interventions on performance: a historical review, a meta-analysis, and a preliminary feedback intervention theory. *Psychological Bulletin*, 119(2): 254–84.

Layton, D. (1991) Science education and praxis: the relationship of school science to practical action, *Studies in Science Education*, 19: 43–79.

Marshall, B. (2000) *English Teachers – The Unofficial Guide: Researching the Philosophies of English Teachers*. London: Routledge/Falmer.

McCallum, B., McAlister, S., Gipps, C. and Brown, M. (1993) Teacher assessment at Key Stage 1, *Research Papers in Education*, 8(3): 305–27.

Mercer, N. (2000) *Words and Minds*. London: Routledge.

National Research Council (1999) *How People Learn: Bridging Research and Practice*. Washington, DC: National Academy Press.

National Writing Project (1989) *Writing and Learning*. Walton-on-Thames: Thomas Nelson.

National Writing Project (1990a) *Audiences for Writing*. Walton-on-Thames: Thomas Nelson.

National Writing Project (1990b) *Writing Partnerships 1: Home, School and Community*. Walton-on-Thames: Thomas Nelson.

Newman, R.S. and Schwager, M.T. (1995) Students' help seeking during problem solving: effects of grade, goal, and prior achievement, *American Educational Research Journal*, 32(2): 352–76.

OFSTED (1996) *Subjects and Standards: Issues for School Development Arising from OFSTED Inspection Findings 1994–5*. London: HMSO.

Perrenoud, P. (1991) Towards a pragmatic approach to formative evaluation, in P. Weston (ed.) *Assessment of Pupils' Achievement: Motivation and School Success*, pp. 79–101. Amsterdam: Swets and Zeitlinger.

Perrenoud, P. (1998) From formative evaluation to a controlled regulation of learning processes: towards a wider conceptual field, *Assessment in Education*, 5(1): 85–102.

Pimm, D. (1987) *Speaking Mathematically*. London: Routledge and Kegan Paul.

Radnor, H.A. (1994) The problems of facilitating qualitative formative assessment in pupils, *British Journal of Educational Psychology*, 64: 145–60.

Reeves, J., McCall, J. and MacGilchrist, B. (2001) Change leadership: planning, conceptualization and perception, in J. Macbeath and P. Mortimore (eds) *Improving School Performance*, pp. 122–37. Buckingham: Open University Press.

Robertson, P. and Toal, D. (2001) Extending the quality framework, in J. Macbeath and P. Mortimore (eds) *Improving School Performance*, pp. 102–21. Buckingham: Open University Press.

Ross, M., Radnor, H., Mitchell, S. and Bierton, C. (1993) *Assessing Achievement in the Arts*. Buckingham: Open University Press.

Rowe, M.B. (1974) Wait time and rewards as instructional variables, their influence on language, logic and fate control, *Journal of Research in Science Teaching*, 11: 81–94.

Ruiz-Primo, M.A., Schultz, S.E., Li, M. and Shavelson, R.J. (2001) Comparison of the validity and reliability of scores from two concept-mapping techniques, *Journal of Research in Science Teaching*, 38(2): 260–78.

Sadler, R. (1989) Formative assessment and the design of instructional systems, *Instructional Science*, 18. 119–41.

Sadler, R. (1998) Formative assessment: revisiting the territory, *Assessment in Education*, 5(1): 77–84.

Shepard, L.A. (1995) Using assessment to improve learning, *Educational Leadership*, 52(5): 38–43.

Shepard, L.A., Flexer, R.J., Hiebert, E.J., Marion, S.F., Mayfield, V. and Weston, T.J. (1994) Effects of introducing classroom performance assessments on student learning, in *Proceedings of the Annual Meeting of the AERA conference*, New Orleans (available from ERIC ED 390918).

Shepard, L.A., Flexer, R.J., Hiebert, E.J., Marion, S.F., Mayfield, V. and Weston, T.J. (1996) Effects of introducing classroom performance assessments on student learning, *Educational Measurement Issues and Practice*, 15(3): 7–18.

Shulman, L. (1986) Those who understand: knowledge growth in teaching, *Educational Researcher*, 15(1): 4–14.

Swain, J.R.L. (1988) GASP: the graded assessments in science project, *School Science Review*, 70(251): 152–8.

Torrie, I. (1989) Developing achievement based assessment using grade related criteria, *Research in Science Education*, 19: 286–90.

Tunstall, P. and Gipps, C. (1996) 'How does your teacher help you to make your work better?' Children's understanding of formative assessment, *The Curriculum Journal*, 7(2): 185–203.

White, B.Y. and Frederiksen, J.T. (1998) Inquiry, modeling and metacognition: making science accessible to all students, *Cognition and Instruction*. 16(1): 3–118.

Wiliam, D. (2001) *Level Best? Levels of Attainment in National Curriculum Achievement*. London: Association of Teachers and Lecturers.

Wiliam, D. and Bartholomew, H. (2001) The influence of ability-grouping practices on student achievement in mathematics, paper presented at the *British Educational Research Association 27th Annual Conference*, University of Leeds, September.

Wiliam, D., Lee, C., Harrison, C. and Black, P. (in press) Teachers developing assessment for learning: impact on student achievement, *Assessment in Education*.

Wood, D. (1998) *How Children Think and Learn: The Social Contexts of Cognitive Development*, 2nd edn. Oxford: Oxford University Press.

Wood, D., Bruner, J.S. and Ross, G. (1976) The role of tutoring in problem solving, *Journal of Child Psychology and Psychiatry*, 17: 89–100.

Further information about publications and other resources can be obtained on the King's website in the pages of the King's Formative Assessment Group. Some of the publications can be downloaded from this site. The address is: http://www.kcl.ac.uk/depsta/education/research. These pages include references to other useful websites.

Index

INVESTIGATING FORMATIVE ASSESSMENT

Harry Torrance and John Pryor

- How do teachers assess the ordinary classroom work of young children?
- How do pupils understand and respond to that assessment – does it help or hinder their development?
- How can classroom assessment be developed to be more effective in assisting the learning process?

This book brings together various perspectives from the fields of assessment policy development, theories of learning and the sociology of the classroom. The book explores how the assessment of young children is carried out in classrooms and with what consequences for their understanding of schooling and the development of their learning in particular subject areas. The book is based on extensive video and audio tape recordings of classroom assessment 'incidents' along with interviews of teachers and pupils about the process of assessment.

Contents
Introduction – Defining and investigating formative assessment – Teachers' perceptions of 'teacher assessment' – Classroom assessment and the language of teaching – The power of assessment: appropriating children's responses for learning or social control? – Formative assessment and learning: where psychological theory meets educational practice – Ask a genuine question, get a genuine answer – Constructing and integrating assessment and learning – Formative classroom assessment: prospects for improvement – References – Index.

192pp   0 335 19734 5 (Paperback)

openup
ideas and understanding
in social science

www.**openup**.co.uk

Browse, search and
order online

Download detailed
title information and
sample chapters*

*for selected titles

www.**openup**.co.uk